# Chapter One

Today the United States is in trouble. The Federal Government is out of control, special interests, corporations, wealthy individuals, and lobbyists dominate. Politicians run wild while they run the country and decide what is best for their careers. Political gridlock rules the day and the Congress is incapable of passing legislation. The President and the Congress are stalemated into a fierce partisan gridlock while the country suffers enormous problems. Millions of Americans are looking on helplessly as they fear that there is no way for things to get better. People around America and throughout the world wonder if America can do anything anymore. They see an America in steep decline that lacks the ability to govern itself. Some have wondered whether an authoritarian alternative such as Chinas is a superior political and economic system. In America and around the rest of the free world, representative government seems to be in a funk. Europe, Japan and America all seem to be in decline while authoritarian alternatives such as China are hailed as the ideal future of the world. Some may question whether democracy stands any chance in the 21$^{st}$ century.

Yet in all fairness democracy has never actually been tried anywhere in the modern world. America is a republic and was founded as one. The system was created to be a representative form of government. Our system allows the political parties to run the government and decide what is best for their party over what is best for their country. Our system allows Congressman to serve an unlimited number of terms so they can stay in Washington forever working for their largest campaign contributors. Our system does not give the American people a seat at the table in Washington. Our system allows the politicians, special interests, corporations, lobbyists and the wealthy to have far too much power. These groups only represent their narrow private interests even if it is at the expense of the country and the majority of the American people. The people suffer while these powerful organized forces control our government. The people and their problems are left neglected at best and when the politicians try to makc things better they just make things worse in the present political situation. The American people are left adrift in our society. Disillusioned and with a government that is not responsive to their needs or concerns while other more organized and powerful forces out maneuver them.

Americans are increasingly cynical about their government along with their overall prospects in American society. The government has become more powerful, but not to the benefit of the people but at the expense of the people. The government has commanded a larger and larger role in our lives but that has resulted in the benefit of the corporations, unions, political parties, politicians, wealthy individuals and the numerous other special interests. The American people are left neglected with their pockets getting picked clean and their interests ignored. Laws are being passed that outright harm them while benefiting the special interest groups. Some Americans feel like they are rearranging the deck chairs on the Titanic calling the captain to avoid the iceberg dead ahead. Like the captain, the federal government is charting America on a course to ruin and the American people cannot do anything to stop it.

For those still reading do not despair, there is hope for a better alternative. In this book I will outline a series of steps that America could take in order to become a democracy. Those steps include creating a direct democracy, getting rid of the United States Senate, imposing term limits on members of Congress, for federal judges to be subjected to elections and term limits, for the Federal Reserve to be subjected to elections and term limits, to eliminate the Electoral College, for political parties to hold their primary for President on the same day, increase the number of representatives in the House of Representatives and to take redistricting out of politicians hands. In order to put these ideas into practice I will outline how that can be achieved at the end of the last chapter. These ideas are by no means all of the ideas that should be considered, they are a starting place and the theme of this book is that the American people should have control over their own government. They should be the ones who have the ultimate say over what kind of a relationship that they want to have with the federal government. People could like all of these ideas or none of these ideas, but the point of this book is to advocate on behalf of the American people. They have a lopsided relationship with a Washington that has far too much power and that is out of touch. The American people will only have a more balanced relationship if they demand it.

In the founding of the country there was an issue that needed to be solved before every colony would ratify the new US Constitution. Colonies with smaller populations like Georgia, Connecticut and South Carolina were concerned about joining a new country where colonies with larger populations like Virginia, New York and Pennsylvania would dominate. To solve this problem a compromise was arrived at. The Congress would consist of a House of Representatives based off of population and then a Senate, which would give the states equal representation. There was the issue of having coequal branches of the federal government, the Executive branch, legislative branch and the judicial branch. Finally there was the issue of the states versus the federal government. The states were strong during the beginning of Americas history and the federal government was weak. The founding of the country was not about creating a democracy; it was about creating a republic with strong states and a weak federal government. Yet the founders did not give the American people a check against their federal government. They did not believe in democracy, but they did not believe in a strong federal government either. They could have never foreseen the massive increase in the size of the federal government and the centralized authority in Washington. Americans deserve an increase in their power at least commensurate with how much more powerful the federal government has become. The federal government has become far more powerful while the American people have less power and are less free.

In a republic organized groups who possess a large amount of money or resources will always influence politicians. If a special interest group can provide a large amount of money and a large number of votes to a politician, the politician will do what those groups pay them to do. The average person does not possess that kind of power. Just one special interest group will provide the money and votes a politician needs to get elected. The politicians will pay lip service to us or to you if you meet them in person. We do not have the ability individually to help them get elected so they will lobby special interest groups and organizations that do have that ability. Our system allows special interests, lobbyists, corporations, wealthy individuals and others to heavily influence the Congress. Politicians need money to win elections and to keep getting re-elected. If they refuse to work for special interests they will lose the money and the money will go to a political rival of theirs instead. It's a matter of survival for politicians to constantly campaign for campaign contributions along with lining up with the key groups of their political party. Serving their constituents is low on the agenda for every politician in Washington by necessity. A republic is a system where politicians get elected and represent the views of their constituents. They represent their party and their political parties interests as well. These are the two masters that every politician has to deal with. They also have interest groups that fund their campaign. The politicians themselves are constantly evaluating their political life and future as well. These all represent competing interests for a politician. The safe thing for a politician to do is to pay the most attention to his or her own political carriers. That means towing the party line, playing aggressive partisan politics and working for their campaign contributors. Constituents only see their politicians when they make the cheesy photo ops with average people in their districts when an election is imminent. Once the election has taken place those politicians disappear as quickly as they appeared.

The competing motivations, agendas, and influence of these different groups make the politician bend to a lot of factors. They must appease their constituents in order to get re-elected. In order to get their job in the first place they need to be nominated by a political party. Its either the Democratic or Republican parties, but sometimes a candidate runs as a third party or unaffiliated. After receiving a nomination from a party, the person must raise as much money as possible to get elected. More money means more advertising dollars, a larger organization to run the campaign, and more money for paid staff. More money also means enabling larger turnout and generating more support. The candidate that lacks money or major party support is doomed to lose. Only those that can get nominated by a major party and attract high levels of donations can have a chance to get elected. If you go up against the values, philosophy, and interests of either party, you will never get elected to dog catcher much less to Congress. These two parties control the United States government. This makes it impossible to bring in somebody new who would go against the agenda and special interests of each major political party.

A candidate that manages to get through the gauntlet of a primary, raising money and getting elected then has another job. Once elected, the politician has a tight rope to walk. They must appease their party and tow the party line or they will lose their next primary nomination to someone else who will. The politician also must appease the special interests that gave them money to get elected. If they do not those special interests will give their money to someone else who will. The politician must appease the voters from their party who votes for them. If they displease those voters from their party those voters will nominate someone else who will. The politician has to appease these different supporters or they will be out of the job. All politicians have a basic need for a job; the politicians that remain in power are those that appease their supporters. The ones that attempt to do otherwise will lose their political power and ability to do anything. The politician is thinking about their own career, they all want to climb as high up the political ladder as possible. All politicians wake up every morning seeing a President in the mirror. That will prevent them from making decisions or votes that will put their political lives in jeopardy. These realities will prevent the politician from making deals with those of the other party. The politicians own ambition will work to limit how much they are willing to do for their own constituents. The average person does not get their interests and agendas through as a consequence.

The way that things are run in America must change. It's been said before that the only cure for the ills of democracy is more democracy. This book aims to detail some of the steps that the United States could take to transform itself into a democracy and to give the American people ultimate control over their federal government. The only answer is for the American people to have a say in how the country is run, the American people should have a democracy. A lot of people say that we are a democracy but we are not. America is and always has been a republic. We elect people to represent us in Congress and we elect the President to run the executive branch. Not all Americans have even been allowed to do that much for most of American history. This is not what a democracy looks like. One major change that would make America into an actual democracy is by creating what is called a direct democracy. A direct democracy is a system where the American people can vote on issues that they present to the country. The American people would be able to come up with an idea, come up with enough signatures to get that idea on the federal ballot and then if a majority of the people votes yes it becomes law. If a majority of the people vote no, then it does not become law. This would be a simple yes or no vote, majority rules. The special interests, political parties and politicians would not get to be the sole deciders of the national agenda any longer. The American people can finally have a say in the direction of their country. They will no longer have to let special interests control their government. They will no longer have to compromise with the ways of Washington. They will no longer have to wait for the right politician to come along and for the right political circumstances to emerge for them to get what they want. Americans have always called their country a democracy. It's a well-established feature of our society to support democracy or the idea that majority rules. The American culture is much more democratic than our actual system of government is. The changes outlined in this book would put the American people in charge of their government. The best part of the US Constitution is the beginning, "We the People…"

There are 25 states that have a direct democracy or ballot measure system already. That has allowed the people to have more control over their state government. A direct democracy would have an even greater impact with the federal government. The federal government is so large, powerful and influential in our lives. They reign supreme over all of the states and especially over the people. In the beginning, the federal government was weak and the states were strong. Our republic was about empowering the states because the states had to agree to join the United States. Once they joined the union over time the federal government has become larger and stronger. Now the federal government is large and all-powerful, it does not just dominate the United States it dominates most of the world. The American people are left wondering whether they have created some kind of a Frankenstein that they can no longer control. The federal government has given itself promotion after promotion over the years, now it is time for the American people to receive one. The American people need control over a federal government that has unprecedented control over them.

For a direct democracy there would be a certain number of valid signatures in order for a proposed law to qualify for the federal ballot. Let's say that number was equal to one percent of eligible voters in the country. If the proposed law received that number of signatures then it would be on the ballot. This vote would take place every two years when you vote for your member of the House of Representatives. For a law to pass it has to get on the federal ballot. If that proposed law were to receive a majority of the popular vote, then it becomes federal law. There would be three ways for a law to be repealed. The first would be if another ballot measure were to receive enough signatures so it could get on the ballot, then it receives a majority of votes cast to eliminate that law. The second way a law could be repealed would be if two thirds of the House of Representatives voted to eliminate that law (This is assuming there is no US Senate). No President would have veto power over any law passed by the American people. The third way would be if there was a challenge to the US Supreme Court as to whether the law passed was Constitutional or not. Another option that the people would have would be for the American people to consider multiple proposals at the same time. Instead of only being able to make a yes or no decision, the people could offer more nuanced answers. For example lets say that one group makes a healthcare reform proposal, then two other groups make different healthcare reform proposals. The American people would have three completely different healthcare reform proposals to consider. The healthcare reform proposal that received the highest number of votes would become law. This would not require a majority of the votes, it would only require winning the most votes. In this instance the people would be able to have multiple choices and have more control than a simple yes or no vote. Some proposed laws are binary decisions where a yes or no decision makes sense, in other cases the American people could consider multiple different proposals at the same time and decide what they like best. A direct democracy would be the biggest change America could make in order to become a democracy. There are others changes that would further reduce the power of the federal government and give it to the people.

The next piece of reform that would make America more democratic would mean removing the United States Senate. It's not democratic that each state has two senators. A Senator from Wyoming is representing a state of around half a million people, while the Senator from California is representing a state of around forty million people. Does that representation seem fair to you? Removing the Senate would be a large change to the federal government and how the Congress is structured. The states are all equally represented in the Senate and that body was created to assure that all states would be equally represented. If the Senate were to go, it would take power away from the Congress and the states and give it to the people. The Senate is inherently undemocratic. Each state gets two Senators each, they get to serve six-year terms, which is two years longer than the President gets. They can also serve indefinitely; there are no term limits for Senators. The House of Representatives more closely represents the will of the people and Representatives in the House serve for two-year terms. Since the House is based off of population it more accurately reflects the peoples will than the Senate. The Senate is more corrupted by party and special interests than the House of Representatives is.

8

The Senate presides over the country nearly oblivious to the electorate, which is not democratic at all. If there were just a House of Representatives then it would equally represent the people as opposed to equaling representing the states. The Senate was created to make sure each state was represented equally in Congress. The time where that was necessary to bring states into the union has long passed. The House of Representatives was created to represent the people, making that the only body in Congress would make it easier to pass legislation and to carry out what the people want. The Senate does not represent the people as well as the House. Senators are more beholden to the states and special interests. Not to mention, a piece of legislation has to go through the House and the Senate to arrive at the Presidents desk for a signing or a veto. To make things more democratic and efficient the House of Representatives could be the only body that legislation has to pass through in the Congress.

The next change that would make the country more democratic would be for the members of the Congress to have term limits. It would enable new people to get elected to Congress who would have more of the people's interests at heart. It would prevent a career politician from staying in power for decades serving their party and special interests while ignoring their constituents. This would create a more short-term politician who would spend more time appeasing their constituents than appeasing their backers. Term limits would attract people that wanted to serve their constituents rather than their own political career. Less time in Congress would make it more difficult for Representatives to be captured by special interests. Having a lot of new people serving in Congress regularly would make it more difficult for special interests to buy congressman. The people would benefit by regularly sending somebody new from their district to Washington. The jobs in Congress would have regular openings so an average citizen could participate in their own government. It would assure that the people had a Representative who most understood their lives and concerns. A member can stay in Washington for too long and become out of touch with their constituents. They end up making Washington the place where they spend most of their time. The term-limited politician would have a temporary stay in Washington rather than it being their new home.

The next change that would make the country more democratic would be to have term limits and elections for federal courts. Each member of the court is nominated by the President and confirmed by the United States Senate. This represents two problems. One problem is that a President and the Senate choose who serves on the Supreme Court and other federal courts. The politicians have political leanings; they insist on litmus tests for potential Supreme Court justices. It's partisan to have these people selecting a member of the Supreme Court. To take the decision making out of their hands would increase the judiciaries independence. The second problem with federal judges is that they have no term limits. Once the U.S. Senate that's it confirms them, the justices are on the federal bench for life. Often a lot of them have lived out their lives on the court. There should be term limits for members of the federal courts. They are barely accountable to the people in the first place much less when they have a life term on the Supreme Court. Term limits would constantly bring new people to the federal judiciary and it would give more people a chance to serve. We should elect members of the Supreme Court to staggered four-year terms with a maximum of two terms allowed. If the President can only be there for two terms of four years each, why can a Justice on the Supreme Court be there longer much less for life? Justices for the Supreme Court and all federal courts should be elected. It wouldn't be up to the President and Senate who got to serve as a federal judge. For such a powerful institution, the federal courts are not responsible to the people at all. Term limits and elections would allow more people to serve as federal judges and give the people some control over the judiciary. It would not compromise the independent judiciary; there are state court judges elected all over the country.

The next piece of reform that would make the United States more democratic would be to subject members of the Federal Reserve to elections and term limits. The Federal Reserve is arguably the fourth branch of the federal government. It is an institution that is 100 years old and has had a larger impact on the US economy than any other organization in the country. Yet this powerful institution is not even in the US Constitution. The members of the board of governors are selected by the President and confirmed by the Senate. The American people should elect those that serve in the Federal Reserve districts and in the board of governors. Private banks get to decide who serves on regional Federal Reserve boards. The power that private banks, Wall St. and Congress have should go to the American people. Opening up the process to elections would allow a greater variety of people to serve and give the American people the final say. It would require the Federal Reserve to defend their policies to the American people. It would require the Fed to become more transparent about their operations and their intentions. The American people would be able to make sure that the Federal Reserve was conducting monetary policy that was to the benefit of the economy as opposed to the narrow private interests of banks and Wall Street. Elections would allow the people to elect candidates that would have no chance of getting onto the Federal Reserve boards. Elections and term limits would not compromise the Feds independence; sound Fed policy generally benefits the American economy and the American people. The current Federal Reserve has too much independence where they are captured by private banks and their private interests. The American people deserve control over their own government and deserve a Federal Reserve that sets monetary policy to the benefit of America at large. The very economic fortunes of every American is closely tied in with Fed policy, this institution is far too powerful and misunderstood to be left entirely independent of the American people.

The next change that would be made to make America more democratic would be if the Electoral College were done away with. Most of the time it has been consistent with who has won a majority of the popular vote for President. In 1876, 1888 and 2000, this was not the case. The candidate that won a majority of the popular vote for President lost the election to the candidate that won the Electoral College. The Electoral College is undemocratic and unfair. It's unfair because it leads to candidates winning the Presidency who lose the popular vote. It's also unfair because it causes the two leading candidates for President to focus on a small number of states instead of the entire country. There are so called swing states that determine who is elected President, they are the states that have the Electoral College votes to make someone President. They are states such as Ohio, Florida, Virginia, North Carolina, Michigan, Pennsylvania, Wisconsin, Virginia, Iowa, New Mexico, Nevada, Colorado, Indiana and New Hampshire. These are the states that decide Presidential elections in the United States. If we had no Electoral College then the Presidential candidates would be free to campaign in other parts of the country too. They would be free to run more of a national campaign instead of one that is directed at voters in these states. It's odd that when you look at California and Texas, the two most populous states in the US, they are basically ignored during the Presidential election. It's also states with small populations like Alaska, Hawaii, Vermont, Wyoming, Nebraska, Delaware, Rhode Island and others that are ignored. Other states with large populations like Georgia, Washington, New Jersey, Massachusetts, and New York are ignored too. A majority of the country is not catered to at best and ignored at worst during a Presidential election. Having an Electoral College is also unnecessary. In all Presidential elections except three, has the Electoral College vote lined up with the popular vote. We no longer need the Electoral College. We should get rid of the Electoral College to prevent someone in the future from winning the Electoral College while losing the popular vote and becoming President. More importantly we should do away with the Electoral College so the candidates can run a truly national campaign. Not an election that is decided by a relatively small group of swing voters in a small number of swing states.

In addition to getting rid of the Electoral College, political parties need to hold their primary for President on the same day. For the Democratic and Republican parties Iowa is the first state that holds its caucus, the next state is New Hampshire which technically has the first primary for President, the third state in line is South Carolina. These states get to decide who the Presidential nominees are for both major parties, or they greatly reduce the number of candidates running. Candidates who perform poorly in these early states run out of money and leave the race. The candidate who wins these early primaries usually has unstoppable momentum and goes on to win their parties nomination for President. The Democratic and Republican parties should hold a national primary on the same day. Whatever candidate receives the highest number of votes becomes their parties nominee for President. It would give Democrats and Republicans all over the country an equal opportunity to decide who their parties nominee was. It would allow a greater variety of people to win their parties nomination than would be possible today. It would be a more fair and democratic process if everyone had the chance to participate.

Another reform that would make America more democratic would be to take redistricting out of the hands of politicians. There should be a non-partisan committee that creates the districts and then the proposal goes before the voters for final approval. With a Republic the politicians answer to those that are the most responsible for getting them elected. They do not answer to their constituents or the people they are supposed to represent. They do as little as they have to in order to get re-elected. It's not just the political parties, special interests and voters that keep a politician around, it's also their voting districts that keep them in power. Most congressional districts are created by the state legislature. The politicians that run the state legislature are the ones that create each congressional district. If that district is created so that a majority of the voters that live there vote for one political party, it's next to impossible to get rid of that politician. The politicians in the legislature are of the same political party as those running for Congress, yet they get to create the congressional districts. Isn't this a brazen conflict of interest? They will create districts that will allow their party to control as many seats in Congress as possible, not what serves their citizens best.

If a committee of non-partisan people created the districts and the voters could make the final decision, it would take the decision out of the hands of politicians and solve the conflict of interest issue. With a party in charge of creating congressional districts it is free to make them however they want. That means they will create a district where the majority of people in that district are registered voters of their party. That makes the seat easy for the incumbent Congressman to keep. It also makes it nearly impossible for a member of the other party to win that seat. For a party in charge of the legislature they get to decide what the congressional districts look like after the census. The census takes place every ten years. At the beginning of each new decade a federal census takes place. After the census is tallied the members of the legislature get to do what is called redistricting. The political party who has the majority of seats in the legislature gets to decide what each congressional district looks like. They can change the districts so that districts that once were divided or safe for the other party can be made safe for their party and candidates. This is a process that makes the country less democratic. It allows political parties and politicians to limit the people's choices and will. This represents a serious conflict of interest problem. This makes it easy for a Congressman to be in Congress for decades and never face serious opposition. Even if they do a poor job it will be nearly impossible for that person to lose. If a congressional district has more registered Republicans than Democrats, then that district will be majority Republican. As long as that politician appeases the Republican Party, his special interests and makes some voting decisions that make people in his district happy, he or she will stay there for as long as they want to. It's very difficult to remove a politician that is in a district where a majority of the people are voters in the politician's party. Only if the politician makes voters in their party unhappy or by making a huge personal mistake do they risk losing their seat. Each party does this in all fifty states.

Another idea that would lead to a more democratic United States would be to increase the number of representatives in the House of Representatives. Today there are only 435 representatives representing some 300 million people. The number of representatives has not changed in nearly a century. While the population is so much greater than it used to be, the American population is three times larger now than it was 100 years ago. There are obvious limits to the number of representatives needed to serve the people well, yet there could easily be twice as many representatives in Congress as there is now. There is also the problem with representation. The Wyoming representative represents around half a million people in their state. There are representatives who represent a million people and some who represent a five hundred thousand people. This is unfair to constituents; the representatives should represent a similar number of people. In order to make that possible there should be a larger number of representatives in Congress. Issues of representation in Congress is tied in with redistricting. If the redistricting process were changed, it would give the people more control over the congressional districts that they live in. The people would be able to prevent congressman from serving in politically safe districts. Having a higher number of representatives and taking the decision about redistricting out of politicians hands would give the people more control over their representative in Congress. That would make Congress more democratic and responsive to their constituents. In order to make the country more based off of the will of the American people, there should be a higher number of representatives. This would allow the people to be represented more evenly and create more politicians representing the voters interest in Congress. Increasing the number of representatives and taking redistricting decisions out of politicians hands would make the country more democratic.

These are ideas that represent a large change in America. These ideas would make the United States more democratic. It would put more control and power in the hands of the American people instead of political parties, politicians, corporations, special interests and other forces that work to get their interests through at the expense of the public welfare. The American people are the ones who own this country. They are the ones who are the most affected by the laws passed in Washington D.C. They are the ones who bear the burdens of the laws passed more than anyone. Yet the American people have the least amount of say in whether laws are passed in the first place, much less what kind of laws are passed. Politicians, political parties, and special interests are literally in the room when laws are being written. They get to decide how laws look and whom they apply to. They also get to decide who are exempted from laws. The American people have no seat at the bargaining table for how laws are actually written. Our interests and wishes are not at the top of the agenda, much less on the agenda at all.

Americans have always believed that this is a democracy and at some level it is. It is not with the Federal government. We have a republic, we elect members of the House and the Senate, we also elect the President every four years and yet we have no actual control over the federal government. Politicians win elections and that's when they forget about the people or their constituents entirely. Politicians go to Washington to make deals. They will do everything they can to get re-elected and stay in power for the rest of their lives. Yet it is not as straightforward as you would think. Members of the Congress have a lot of people to work for before they even think of working for their constituents or voters. They have their special interests, they have their political parties, they have their largest financial donors to their campaign and they have their own political careers to worry about. American voters are literally at the bottom of the list of those things that politicians care about.

If you are in a congressional district or state where the majority of voters are Democrat. Then your Representative or Senator will more than likely be a Democrat. If you are a Democrat, even then your concerns will be low on the politician's list of who to appease in Washington. If you are a Republican in a district or state like this then you will have very minimal representation in Congress. You are at the very bottom of whom your Congressperson or Senator is trying to appeal to. You will have virtually none of your views represented in Washington D.C. The opposite is also true. If you live in a congressional district or state that is majority Republican, then your Representative or Senator will more than likely be a Republican. If you are a Republican then your views will be expressed but even then you will lose out to special interests, the Republican Party and the politician. If you are a Democrat then you especially will have next to no voice in Congress. If you don't identify with either party no matter where you live, you will find yourself disenfranchised. You will not have a member of the

16

House or a Senator who will express your views and will be beholden to you. In this situation you are at the bottom of the pile. You are the person who is the least represented all over the country. You may be the most sought after voter in election after election but members of political parties are better represented. Why deal with all of these different people in the first place? Politicians, political parties, special interest groups, wealthy contributors, corporations, members of political parties, it all depends on where you live. All of these different groups of people and interests are in line ahead of you. The politician will tell you that you are their largest concern and interest yet that is not true. You are the person that they are the least interested in helping.

With this situation there is a solution, there are a number of solutions. These changes would make America democratic and would give the people the influence and control that they deserve. The problem is that the American people lack the ability to take problems into their own hands. They must make compromises with the powers in Washington before anything can get done. The American people would able to decide what they wanted to vote on, and decide yes or no if it becomes law or not. They could be presented with multiple proposals at the same time and decide what they liked best. Passing legislation and reforming the country would not be reserved for Congress and the President any longer. The people would be able to decide a large number of issues that cannot or will not be taken care of by the federal government. Not only would a direct democracy empower the people to take action, it would also empower the people to stop the federal government from doing something they do not approve of. It would give the American people a lot more control over what the Congress is allowed to do and what it is not allowed to do. More democracy would not only be a gas pedal or a brake for the people, it would also take money and power out of Washington and put it back in the hands of the people. Lobbyists, corporations, political parties, politicians, special interests and others would be forced to work more with the people. They would have to spend less money on politicians and more money on trying to influence the American public. The typical Congressional deals would be brought into the daylight with public scrutiny. There would be fewer back room deals that benefit those in power. This increased level of transparency along with making the special interests cater to the public would improve the lives of the average American. Don't even begin to feel like this book has all of the answers, this is a starting point for a more democratic country. This book will go into more detail on the above ideas in the coming chapters. The final chapter will discuss two possible ways that these ideas could actually happen.

# Chapter Two

One of the main ideas of this book is that America should adopt a direct democracy, that would be a crucial ingredient for the United States to become a democracy. That change would allow the people to propose a law, collect enough valid signatures to qualify for the federal ballot and then the voters say yes or no to the proposed law. They would have the option of weighing multiple proposals at the same time and whatever proposal received the highest number of votes would become law. Direct democracy allows the American people to pass legislation without having to deal with Congress and the President. It would be up to the American people once and for all what sort of relationship that they want to have with the Federal Government. Politicians, political parties, lobbyists, special interest groups, corporations, wealthy individuals would no longer have a monopoly on creating laws. A direct democracy would allow the people to reign in these power brokers along with Washington in general. America would finally become a real, genuine democracy with this addition to our political system.

The American people deserve to have the ultimate say. People shouldn't only get to decide who represents them in Congress or who the President is. The people don't have much of a choice when it comes to who those people are anyway. The American people should have a say in crafting laws and be able to vote on them independently of the Federal Government. We should not have to wait in line behind special interests, corporations, lobbyists, political parties, politicians, and everyone else ahead of us. America should be free of the corrupting influences of these different people and groups. They have their own agendas and interests at stake. They are spending lots of money every year to make sure that their interests are served in Congress. The politicians have to serve those paying them instead of being free to do what the people want. Politicians also have their own political leanings as well as their political career to worry about. They will not vote for anything that will imperil those things. The interests of the people are served last if at all. We should not have to compromise with those interests and the process of Washington. The American people deserve better than that.

The direct democracy system would serve us better than the status quo. It has been called a ballot measure system, initiative, referendum, direct initiative, popular referendum and a direct democracy, they all mean the same thing and it is a straight forward proposition. A person or group comes up with an idea that they would like to make into a law. For their idea to get on the federal ballot it would require a certain number of people signing their name on a petition to get it on the ballot. In most states that have a ballot measure already it requires signatures from anywhere from four to eight percent of recent voters to get a measure on the ballot. A rule could require something like this percent of eligible voters to sign a petition in order for it to get on the federal ballot. After the signatures are verified as being legitimate signatures then the proposed law would qualify for the federal ballot. Once it was on the federal ballot there would be an election on the first Tuesday of November. An election would take place every two years, as often as representatives in Congress are elected. For a proposed law to pass it would require a majority of voters to vote in favor of it. If a proposed law failed to receive a majority of the vote then it would fail to pass. This is a simple way of allowing the American people to decide. They would get to decide what laws they wanted and what laws they didn't want. They could vote to overturn existing federal laws or they could vote to approve new federal laws. It would be the American people who could come up with legislation and be the ultimate decider. No longer would Washington hold everybody hostage.

There would be a second way that ballot measures would be dealt with. Besides Yes or No questions voters would be presented with multiple-choice questions. If a proposed law received enough signatures to qualify for the federal ballot then voters could vote to approve or disapprove. In another circumstance groups could create competing proposals that would directly compete with each other instead of it being a simple Yes or No vote. The voters could be presented with multiple different proposals at the same time, these proposals would go head to head with each other rather than being voted on in separate Yes or No votes. One group could get enough signatures for their proposal to get on the federal ballot, a second group gets enough signatures to qualify, a third group and a fourth group does the same thing so their proposals would be up for consideration at the same time. The proposal that received the highest number of votes would become law. There could be competing proposals for health care reform, immigration reform, tax code reform, etc. The voters would be asked to choose between competing proposals. Some ballot measures like "Should marijuana be legal" or "should we ban trans fats" would be Yes or No questions that would be ballot measures with Yes or No options only and other proposed laws would be more complicated. Another possibility is that voters could be awarded more options than just Yes or No; they could be given alternatives to consider instead. The answer that receives the highest number of votes would become law. Voters could decide to either a change proposal, keep things the way they are, a little bit of change or they could opt to adopt part of the proposal as opposed to all of it. This increase in options and complexity would give the voters more choices and better serve the American people by letting them be more specific about what they want. A Yes or No vote only for all proposals would not best serve the people. Not all problems or issues are simple binary situations; the American people should be given additional options to ensure that their wishes are carried out. Giving the voters more options would let more Americans get what they wanted and make for more satisfactory results.

Direct democracy allows America to become democratic and to embrace the principal that majority rules. This is a very simple system, yet it is powerful. It would allow the people to settle a large number of issues that are left unsettled by the federal government. Finally there would be some way of letting the American people decide some very divisive and controversial issues. These are issues that the politicians and political parties use to rile up their base and encourage higher voter turnout. They use the various wedge issues to galvanize their political base to show up and vote on Election Day. A base that is content is a political base that is not likely to show up as much as a base that is scared. Nothing motivates people like fear. The politicians need their political base to turn out so they can win, especially in more competitive districts or swing states. Usually the side that can do a better job of getting their political base to the polls will win the election. This incentivizes the politicians to use any issue they can that excites, angers and or scares their base into showing up and voting for them. The politician needs their base to feel like their very lives and everything they hold sacred depends upon them winning this election. The more they succeed at doing that the more passionate their base will be about showing up and voting on election day. A less interested voter might decide to do something else on Election Day. The politicians on either side or for any party will do whatever they have to in order to win. As a consequence there are too many issues that are used as political footballs. All the while the people suffer and are manipulated by politicians and political parties. We should have a way of settling these sometimes very sensitive issues. The politicians should not be allowed to indefinitely hold these issues and divisions over us for the sake of their own political agendas.

Another large problem that the country faces today is a large degree of political polarization. The Democratic Party is socially liberal and believes in a large role for the federal government. The Republican Party is socially conservative and believes in a limited role for the federal government. The two main parties are complete opposites on nearly every issue so this creates a large wedge in American society that is made up of many individual wedge issues. If you are somebody that does not agree with everything that either party stands for you will not find many other options. If you don't embrace the entire platform you will not be welcomed into either party. You can vote for third party candidates or choose not to vote but this tactic does not succeed very often. This is another problem that the current system does not do an adequate job of addressing. This situation leaves swing voters in the middle left to decide which candidate that they like more or the one that they "would like to have a beer with". It mostly becomes a personality contest or popularity contest as opposed to being about the issues. The voters are not able to decide any issues and they are only able to elect politicians that make a variety of promises. Politicians make all sorts of promises, sometimes they will say anything to get elected and sometimes they earnestly mean what they say yet when elected they are unable or incapable of delivering on those promises. Regardless of why promises are not kept the results are the same. Nothing ever really changes or gets done and this cycle repeats itself every election cycle. The people are in no position to change this situation, all they can do is throw the bums out and replace those bums with new bums. The system needs reforming so the people have control over their government. A direct democracy would allow the people to decide issues. That is part of the reason why the country is so polarized. The people cannot resolve any problems or issues. The politicians and political parties use a large number of issues such as abortion, gay rights, gun control, taxes, the death penalty, and immigration among many other issues to divide the people. They divide the people to get their base of voters out to vote. The more angry and worried people are, the more likely they are to become radicalized and go out to vote. Polarization is a large problem today. While there are political games, gridlock, and fierce partisan games in Washington DC, the people are left divided, angry and disillusioned with the government. The politicians in Washington pay lip service to the idea of bipartisanship. There are some of them that are well meaning; yet there are too many of them that want to play politics instead. These partisan games are a dangerous sideshow these days. The people have real problems and for whatever reason nothing is getting done. If the people could decide what they wanted to vote on and be the deciders as to whether it became law or not we could get around this impasse in Washington. The country has become more and more divided and the federal government seems less and less able to deal with problems. The government seems less and less responsive to the needs and desires of the people. The partisan gridlock and fierce partisanship in the country makes it difficult for interests on each side to get anything done. The current situation makes it nearly impossible to get anything done, even things that have overwhelming political support. Things like getting the spending and federal deficit under control. Having border security. Doing things to get the economy growing fast enough to create tens of millions of jobs again. There are so many things that the people want done that are not getting done. We need to remember that we are all Americans and that we are all in this together. We need to unite against Washington and claim our rightful place in the drivers seat.

There are so many politicians, Presidents, and political parties that have let the people down. They get elected making all kinds of promises about what they will do and all of the problems that they will solve. Then they get sworn in and people realize pretty quickly that they have just elected another placeholder to office. They get too comfortable with the ways of Washington and lose sight of serving the people. Even well meaning politicians go to Washington and are unable to overcome the power brokers and are unable to get anything done. The public is constantly being let down by politicians and presidents who fail. This creates a more disillusioned public that loses faith in the idea that the government can work or that our system can work. If the people had a direct democracy, things could get done. Even if the thing you supported did not receive a majority of the vote you could at least console yourself with the fact that the people decided, the majority ruled the day. It came much closer to becoming law than it ever would have otherwise. The American people always say that majority rules. This is an opportunity to make that a fact and reality in the United States. There are plenty of problems that are left to fester. If the people were able to vote on issues we could decide them once and for all. The country could move on to other issues and have a way of resolving issues that a vast majority of the American people believes in.

It is difficult to leave outstanding issues up to the courts. There are plenty of controversial issues like abortion and gay marriage that have been settled by the Supreme Court. Federal courts are where constitutional and legal issues are decided but those courts are filled with judges and Justices that are appointed by politicians. There are Democrat and Republican judges and justices throughout our legal system. There is a much more stridently partisan aspect to our judicial system than would be expected. It seems less and less about the law and the Constitution and more about what political party was able to have a President appoint more members to the federal judiciary. This hardly seems like a fair way of adjudicating deeply divisive issues. There are some judges that can be trusted to judge fairly and make rulings within the Constitution. There are other judges that are extremely partisan who cannot be trusted to judge fairly. The average American is uncomfortable with being ruled by a bunch of Judges. Even Thomas Jefferson warned the American people of judicial despotism. The courts are a great way to decide many problems in our society. Yet there are issues that are better left to the people themselves. Since federal judges don't have term limits it has the effect of putting very partisan people on the federal bench for decades. Those are people that are putting ideology above the constitution. Instead of several partisan judges getting to decide all of the time we deserve to all vote on whether certain things should be legal or not. We all deserve to have a vote on the most divisive issues in our society.

In the future the people for whatever reason may change their mind about a law. If the people rejected a law today there is a possibility that they would agree to it in later years. The reverse is also true, if the people passed a law that they thought was a good idea one year they may experience or see the negative results of the law and vote to get rid of that law later. Just because a majority of people thought that something was a good idea one year does not mean that they will not think so in the future. This is a very important feature of a direct democracy. If the people change their mind they have the power to get rid of a law or to put a law in place that was a good idea. This is a self-correcting mechanism that is a strong feature of a direct democracy. If a law proves to be unpopular people can get rid of it. Today if a law is passed that becomes unpopular the people have no recourse. If there is a certain tax or federal department that the people favor getting rid of, they are not able to under the status quo. If there is something that they think should become law it cannot unless it gets through the

Congress and President. It is very difficult to create a new law much less get rid of an unpopular one in today's system.

The people deserve to be able to get rid of an unpopular law. The people deserve to be able to pass a popular thing into law. Under the current system it is very difficult for these things to happen. The right cosmic alignment of political interests in Washington has to come together for a popular law to become law. For an unpopular law to be done away with or a government program to be done away with, it is nearly impossible to do so. Especially for a government program or department that has entrenched interests that are present in Congress to protect them. Bureaucracy exists to further its own existence. There is a misaligning of incentives with bureaucracy. If the department does an excellent job of solving or mitigating a problem then the Congress cuts its budget because it's not such a problem anymore. That money is deemed to be used somewhere else where it is needed. However, if the agency does a poor job and the problem gets worse then they will receive a budget increase. Since the problem is getting worse the Congress decides to throw more money at it. If the government agency solves the problem the agency goes away, if the government agency allows the problem to get worse then they will receive a larger budget and more money from Congress. This operates as a major disincentive for a bureaucracy to actually solve any problems. A direct democracy would allow the American people to solve this problem; they would get to decide what federal department existed. They would be in a position to get rid of bureaucracy, government agencies and departments that they don't want or that they feel should be a local or state responsibility. It would change the incentives for the federal departments to do a better job of delivering on their agencies or departments objectives. Direct democracy would realign the bureaucracy with the American people as opposed to them only pursuing what is good for their department. Americans are the ones who understand what they need better than the government ever could. People in Washington are out of touch with the needs of every day people. Bureaucracy and other members of the deep state that are not politicians would finally be reined in with a direct democracy. Every day Americans deserve control over not just the politicians in Washington but the federal bureaucracy in general.

Americans demand common sense solutions passed through consensus. They are unable to pass laws that would help them. Sometimes the Federal Government passes laws that help everyday people. Yet most people cannot remember the last time that happened. There is a great deal of dysfunction in the Capital in addition to the other problems. The people deserve a way of presenting laws and voting on them that does not involve the dysfunction of Washington. A direct Democracy would allow the people themselves to determine what laws they would like passed. If there are enough signatures and it gets on the Federal Ballot, then it requires only a simple majority. This process requires low involvement or input from the power players in Washington. Today, people have a long list of demands that are not being met in Washington. They see corruption, dysfunction and the country suffering. They witness more and more problems in their day-to-day lives that are being ignored and are not being addressed by Washington. People are sick of the excuses and demand action that will address their problems.

If only people could pass laws on their own imagine all of the problems that could be solved. Much less there would be solutions that were not only voted on with a majority of the peoples support but the solutions came from the people too. There would still be some influences from politicians, political parties, and special interests. Yet they would not monopolize power and decision making like they do now. There would not only be issues that would help the average person. Other issues that would be voted on would be much more controversial like gay marriage, legalizing marijuana, abortion, the death penalty, and other wedge issues. There would finally be a forum for the people to decide the fate of these issues. We could stop politicians and political parties from continuing to divide the people along these lines and politicize these issues. It would not simply be left unresolved for these forces to continue to exploit the divide for their own political agenda.

There will be some issues voted on much more controversial than others. But the American people believe in majority rule and the Constitution. The United States Supreme Court is the ultimate legal arbiter in America. There would certainly be legal challenges to some laws that received a majority of votes. That is our process and should be permitted. A direct democracy will not solve all of our problems, yet it is a way we could solve many problems and take control of our own society. The people of this country deserve a way to address their problems. With a President and Congress that don't have a clue. With a large number of special interest groups and political parties that get in the way with their own agendas. There is a great amount of cynicism and disillusionment about the government. People feel as if they are powerless against this system. No matter whether they vote or not or whom they vote for things stay the same. With a direct democracy people could take matters into their own hands. There would be a more direct point in people voting. People would not have to listen to more lofty promises from politicians or more grandstanding from Congress. Some of the politicians are well meaning and lack the ability to get things done. Others are politicians that will say anything to get elected. No matter what kind of politician it is the people are left without any solutions to their problems.

The people are tired of hearing empty promises from politicians. They don't see the point in one politician of one party or one politician of another party getting elected. They don't see any real material differences in their day-to-day lives. It's all a game in Washington and the people are tired of watching politicians playing it. The politicians are fighting over power and influence. All the while special interest groups are using a lot of money and resources to pursue their agendas. There are many groups in Washington that benefit different groups of people and need representation. Yet those groups among other groups pursue their own agendas at the expense of the people as a whole. There are plenty of things that a majority of the people would approve of that do not get made into law in DC. A direct democracy would not eliminate the lobbying aspect of government. Nor would it get rid of the corrosive effects of special interest groups. Yet a direct democracy would do two things for the people. One, it would allow the people to pass laws independently of those powers in Washington. Second, it would allow the people to have a way of curbing or reining in the power of special interest groups, politicians, and political parties.

War is an eventuality. Throughout American history war has been an unpleasant reality for the American people. Especially for the men and women in uniform who fought for our freedoms and liberties. This is a topic that concerns a direct democracy. Should the American people decide if we go to war or not? Should the people decide if we continue fighting a war or not? Under a direct democracy the people would be able to decide if we went to war or not. They could also decide if we stayed in a war. Yet the President and the Congress would have to officially declare war. They would also have the discretion of running the war effort. The people would have to be patient with the war effort and the abilities of the federal government to win that war. War is a very tough and divisive problem that will not go away. At some point in time, war we be a reality. As desirable as peace is war will always happen for one reason or another at some point in time. The people deserve a say in whether a war happens or not, whether we have a draft or not, whether the war continues or not. The people deserve a say in what happens to our nations military and what decides war and peace. However the generals and the President should be free to conduct the war and win whatever war it is. It seems to be tradition in American history that Americans have fewer civil liberties during a time of war. Yet sometimes that is necessary as during the Civil War to protect the country and win the war. It is a difficult task deciding where the line is between the practical necessity of winning a war and the moral issue of civil liberties being respected. The people deserve a say in this difficult debate. Yet that doe's not mean that the people should have no way to make their voices heard. If a war is unpopular the people should be able to pass a ballot measure to express that. The people should also have the right to eliminate the draft. The draft is a serious issue that in some cases the government uses to conduct a war. The people should be able to decide whether their sons and daughters can be drafted to fight a war.

The people should not have to be drafted if majorities of the people vote against the draft. The federal government should have the flexibility to conduct a war even if it is unpopular. Yet the people should not only retain the right to vote against an unpopular war they should be able to take action by getting rid of the draft. Being able to get rid of the draft would certainly be possible if a war was unpopular. It would also put pressure on the government to either end the war or to enact measures to make more people volunteer to fight. War is a difficult and terrible issue and there are times that the country fights in one. Yet even in a direct democracy there are times when it is unwise for the public to be able to determine whether we stay in a war or not. There are times that a war gets unpopular and that it must be won. It would be unwise to tie the hands of future generals. Removing the draft is a compromise that would allow those that objected to the war to not fight. It would allow those that wished to fight to be able to fight. If the government had trouble attracting enough people to fight in a war they would either end it or they would raise the pay of soldiers and or do something else to entice people to volunteer for the military. There has been an all-volunteer military so far since 1973 and it has worked extremely well. Especially when a war was unpopular, the war could be fought to completion as a result of there being no draft. People can have any opinion they want about war, war is hell, yet it is a part of reality and unfortunately must be dealt with some time.

For a ballot measure to get on the federal ballot it would require a certain number of signatures. It could be equal to around four to eight percent of voters as it is done in many states. A simple majority would allow that ballot measure to become law. This is a system that would be easy to implement and would be a democratic addition to our republic. The American people and presidents have always referred to our country as a democracy. Yet we have only been more democratic in some states, at the federal level this country is a republic. Allowing people to draft their own laws attain the required

signatures for it to be on the ballot and then be on the ballot for an up or down vote by the people would

be a direct democracy. This would make the United States a real democracy. Part of the problems that

the country faces is the system of government we have. It is one of the most perfect forms of

government invented in human history so far. Yet an improvement that could take place would be for a

direct democracy to happen. A lot of the problems we have in America are because of our system.

Lobbyists, special interest groups, politicians, political parties, the wealthy, corporations, among others

are the only groups in society at the table in Congress. A vast majority of American society is not

represented in Washington. Our own goals and interests are not being met. If we could have a direct

democracy we could have a mechanism for addressing our own problems. We wouldn't have to wait for

Washington to get with the program.


A direct democracy would allow the people the opportunity to check the power of the interests in

Washington. One of the strengths of the United States government is the idea of checks and balances.

There is the Executive Branch, the Legislative branch, and the Judicial branch. These branches of the

federal government are supposed to be co-equal so they can check each other's power. The Congress, or

the President, or the Supreme Court could be checked by two of the other branches if they became too

powerful. This creates a government where one branch cannot become too powerful. But where are the

peoples check against the federal government? If you do not like what the government in your city is

doing, you can move to a new city. If you do not like what the government in your state is doing you can

move to a different state. If you don't like what the federal government is doing you have few options

outside of leaving the country. Direct democracy would allow the people to have the power to check the

federal government. This is something that the people in America have never had the power to do

before. Throughout most of American history the federal government was small and played no role in

peoples day-to-day lives. Today the federal government plays a larger role than ever in peoples day-to-day lives. The American people should have some way of deciding what the nature of that relationship is. The federal government practically reigns supreme over the American people. Every law they make and regulation they pass supersedes state laws. The American people have no way of making their voices heard. It should not be the federal government that is the most powerful force in America; the American people should be the most powerful force in this country. It shouldn't matter how we are divided, what should matter is that it is up to the American people to decide. The people have had little power to run the country throughout our history. Currently we are at the mercy of the federal government. We have to wait for the perfect person who would make everything right to get elected President. This dream candidate would bring about the laws and reforms that the people wanted. While in reality these kinds of Presidents have been few and far between in American history. We the people deserve a system of government that regularly produces reform that the people want. We should not have to wait for the dream President to come along. We the people are the right people and it is time that we are able to run the country.

Our society is desperate for change and the political process frustrates us. We are frustrated that the federal government cannot solve our problems; we don't feel like we are even being listened to. The politicians continue to play politics and divide us. We have simple requests that the Congress is unwilling to accept. The American people are able to diagnose their countries own problems and come up with solutions. We deserve a way to check the power of the Federal government as well. We deserve the power to do what we want but we also deserve the power to stop what we don't want. The Founders never envisioned a larger federal government that could have such a large impact on people's lives. Now is the time to give the people the ability to decide for themselves what kind of federal government they would like to have. They should not have to make compromises with political parties, politicians, special interests and others. The American people should be in the driver seat of the national agenda. For too many years the people have been an afterthought. The agendas of those in Washington get served while the people lack the ability to get Washington to serve them much less have their voices heard.

For people in America to be able to pass common sense solutions without the interference of the powers that be, a direct democracy would be the answer. The people could decide what they cared about most and put it on the ballot and make it happen. The people would have the ability to stop laws passed in Washington that they disagreed with too. The American people are the ones who bear the burdens of the laws passed in Washington, they cannot carve out exceptions and give their friends exemptions to federal laws like powerful interests can do for themselves. It only makes sense that the people should decide what laws or ideas are up for discussion; much less what actually becomes law. The American people are living in the real world and are the ones who know their own problems best. They know what would help themselves the most. America is a nation of adults we are not a nation of children looking to Washington for guidance. Sometimes there are those in Washington that have great solutions to people's problems. If their ideas are that attractive they should be excited to take their case to the voters. They hide behind closed doors making backroom deals in Washington; direct democracy would bring daylight and transparency to the process. These days the American people are the ones who have the common sense to address their own problems. Not to mention, power, a political career, ideology, party, or special interests do not corrupt the American people. The American people yearn for solutions that they will never get from the status quo. Even if solutions arrive some day, are they solutions most people support? Why do the people have to wait so long for solutions in the first place? Shouldn't the people be allowed to come up with their own solutions to their problems?

The United States would benefit greatly by becoming a direct democracy. It would empower the people, solve problems, and limit the influence of the power brokers in Washington. It would be up to the voters whether something became law or not. The politicians, political parties and special interests would not continue to hold a monopoly on decision making in America. While the power brokers in Washington get their agendas through Congress there are many issues that continue to fester. There are many problems that for one reason or another are not solved and the country is kept in an ideological box. The politicians and political parties exploit these deep partisan divides to enhance their own agendas. They have no desire and no real interest in resolving these issues. They want to hold these issues over the people and motivate their own base to come out and vote for them. The politicians want to play politics with wedge issues by exploiting them to further their own political careers. Whatever side people are on in some of these wedge issues, the American people should not be subjected to politicians who pray on their deepest fears and beliefs to benefit their own political careers. Americans will never be united on all issues, yet what could unite Americans is the idea that we the people should be the ones who get to decide the solutions to our problems.

There are plenty of well meaning politicians and members of special interest groups. If they are that well meaning then they can be on the side of voters deciding their fate. They can be comfortable with taking their case directly to the people. The transparency that comes with that level of democracy should be refreshing and encouraging. If they really believe in their cause they should yearn the opportunity to take their case to the people. The increased transparency would help raise awareness about a variety of problems and issues. Organizations and special interests should crave the ability to make deals with the people in a democracy in an open environment. It is only those that do not wish well for the people who are afraid of an open forum. They outright shun the daylight that would come from appealing to the majority of the American people. A direct democracy would give the people the ability to vote for things that they wanted and to vote against things that they did not want. It would offer up innumerable possibilities that are impossible from a gridlocked Congress. There would not be interference from Washington. They would be forced to hear what the people wanted and for the most part would be forced to accept what the people wanted. When a law passed it would depend on whether the new law was deemed constitutional. It would also depend on whether the Congress decided to veto a law passed by the people, there would be ways for a law passed by the people to be overturned. That may be good or bad but that depends on the issue and the way people decide. A direct democracy is the right thing yet it must be based on the rule of law and most of all the Constitution.

A traditional aspect of the American system of government is the idea of federalism. The idea that the states of the country are sovereign and powerful yet they work with the federal government, which is recognized as the most powerful force in the country. A direct democracy would enable the people to give more power to the states. There are some that feel that the federal government has reigned too supreme in recent years. The whole idea of federalism has seemingly been abandoned. If the people were given power in a direct democracy they would have the power to restore a more traditional relationship between the states and the federal government. A more important aspect that has been missing in American history is the idea that the people are the most important part of society. There is a lot of discussion of the importance of the branches of the federal government and the delicate relationship between them and the states. Yet what has been ignored is the role of individual people. The American Constitution is designed to work for the states and the federal government. There are plenty of freedoms given to the people, yet the people have no particular role in the government. They are not even deemed an equal stakeholder of the government as the federal government and states are. In recent years the power of the federal government and those that influence it are deemed supreme over any other while the people have been forgotten and left behind.

Instituting popular referendum would be a way to get the country on the right track. The American people have the intelligence, decency and common sense to lead their country into a golden age. The people should be able to decide what issues are most important to them and how those issues get solved. The people should be able to veto the Congress and President who does something that lacks a majority of their support. The federal government is not all knowing and certainly should not remain all-powerful. Some doubt whether the American people can be trusted to make decisions in governing their own country. The people are not omnipotent and will not vote in perfect laws all of the time. Yet the people will enact common sense laws most of the time. They will be able to get rid of laws that become unpopular as well. The so-called common person is the largest group in this country. They are the ones who have to live in our society and be the most subjected to laws passed and conditions in the country. They are the ones who lack lobbyists, money, political power, and influence to make the laws. It is these people who are the greatest in number yet have the least amount of power or influence in Washington.

The free market has shown that in individual hands, the economy is more prosperous than if central planners are allowed to control the economy. The capitalist system has spread all over the world; even countries with communist governments like China and Vietnam have adopted capitalism. If capitalism is so effective in general at organizing economic activity, why wouldn't democracy be just as effective in government? After all, capitalism is individual people making decisions that affect the broader economy. If individual people made decisions in a democracy it would have positive implications for the country as well. People have a better sense of what they want than central planners in Washington ever could. The financial crisis and the economy of recent years have made people hate capitalism. It is completely understandable given what happened and given the consequences of the Great Recession. It was corruption and crony capitalism that took place yet nobody went to jail. The Wall Street bailouts were the most disillusioning experience that the people have had with Washington since the Vietnam War. The rich, corporations, and other special interests were served while the average person suffered. The average person paid for the bailout of Wall Street, while they were not helped. This is not a system where the people have control; this is a system where the people are left powerless against politicians, political parties, corporations and other special interests. A genuine democracy would allow the people to control the government and have a real say in what went on and what did not. The average taxpayer was forced to bail out the very banks and financial institutions that were a great deal to blame for the financial crisis and subsequent depression. The banks and financial institutions are wealthier than ever and are prospering while the American people are left with a record national debt, high unemployment and a sluggish economy with dismal prospects. If only the American people were able to vote for the change that they desired. If we had a direct democracy we could vote to help the average American as opposed to the Congress just helping the richest on Wall Street.

A direct democracy would give the American people the ability to decide what laws passed and what did not. Just as capitalism decides what products are sold and what products are not sold. If people do not buy certain products they will not be sold. If they vote with their wallets for example and buy a product it will be around and the company that sells the product will make money. Our entire economy is based off of this idea of consumer led demand. The economy sounds like a theoretical concept but all it is, is us. An economy is the sum of all of the daily decisions that we all make. What stuff do we buy at the store, filling up at the gas station, going to work and getting a paycheck. An economy as large as the United States economy is summing up the actions of over three hundred million people. This also includes all businesses, corporations, government and the net effect of trade. Capitalism is based off of consumer led demand. There is a lot of talk about voting rights, civil rights and other political rights. Economic rights and freedoms are just as important yet they are not discussed too often. The government gives people the right to own private property and engage in capitalism. The government should grant the people more freedom and control over the government. Capitalism is not a system unto itself; it exists because the government gives the people the freedom to engage in it. It's not a perfect system but it has been the most successful way of economically organizing society and creating wealth than any other alternative. Since people are trusted to make their own economic decisions they should be allowed to make their own political decisions too. People can decide where to live, where to work

37

and where to spend their money. People should also be able to decide the laws in our country. If people can be trusted with making their own decisions, they can be trusted with making decisions for society. The average person would not want some other person making all of their economic decisions for them. Communism was based off centrally planned economic activity where the people had zero economic freedoms and rights. If that was such a failure why would central planning be any more effective in government? Why would the average person want the government and those in it to make all of their choices for them either?

When American history is examined it becomes clear that the people in general make good decisions and take care of themselves. The United States became the wealthiest and most powerful nation in history by allowing the average person to run their own life. American society hasn't always been free for everybody, but it has become more free for everyone as time has gone on. Now that women and all people have civil rights (LGBTQ are about too also), it seems to be the appropriate time in American history for direct democracy. It would mark the culmination of a process that saw America in the beginning as a republic with slavery evolving into a genuinely free society with a democracy. The American people don't lack the ability to guide federal policy. Those in the Congress have no fear of losing their seats when very popular laws and ideas do not pass. A direct democracy would allow people the ability to pass popular laws that currently stand no chance of being made into law by the Congress. There are issues like term limits for members of the House and Senate, strong border enforcement, and support for balancing the budget that are never done by the Congress. A direct democracy would allow the people to force those things on the federal government. It would force the federal government to do the things that a majority of the people supported. It would remind them that it is the people who run the country. Today and throughout American history the average person has had limited control over who gets into the Congress and the White House. The average person has had next to no control over what laws are passed in Washington.

Popular referendum would put the American people in the driver seat. They would be able to decide what direction the country would go in for the first time. America is the greatest nation in the history of the world, what makes America exceptional is freedom. It is so rare throughout human history and America is the first free society in human history. Pre-civilization and anarchy is a state of nature where no one has freedom and what Thomas Hobbes describes as "life is cruel, brutish and short". Freedom only exists where it does in the world today because of the United States. One of the things that makes that true is the American people. The people of America certainly have the ability to decide what laws should be passed and what should not be passed. We have the ability to lead America into a new American century. We have the ability to provide another great example to the world. The people could take care of their problems and finally decide long divisive issues like abortion, gay marriage, immigration, taxes, legalizing marijuana, and plenty of other issues. The people could decide what actions they want to take to get the economy going. The people would be able to decide how to guide the country. The people could also decide how they would like to improve the country; their beliefs and ideas could not only be expressed but passed into law. A direct democracy would allow the government to truly represent the people's will and vision. The current situation would not be permitted to continue. The increased public participation in the government would improve our civil society and make people have faith in their government once again.

There is a possibility that for one reason or another the people vote in a law that eventually becomes unpopular. There may be a law that sounds like a good idea at the time to a majority of the people, then the law is implemented and people realize that the law was a bad idea. There are other times that a law would pass and it would not work out as promised and sometimes a law would pass by a small margin in the first place. The people would have the ability to get rid of unpopular laws that they passed. It only makes sense that the people have a way of enacting laws and disposing of laws. Some laws may be good on a temporary basis; other laws may have consequences that were not apparent initially. It's often said that the devil is in the details. There would only be two ways for a law passed by the people to become undone. One way would be for the Congress to vote to overturn the law with two thirds of the House of Representatives and the Senate voting to overturn a law. The second way would be for the US Supreme Court to decide that a law passed was unconstitutional. These are some limited checks that the federal government would have. The President would have no power to overturn the people's will. If neither of these things happened before the next election, then the people could vote to get rid of an unpopular law. For a Congress to gain two thirds of both houses to overturn the peoples will would require some political bravery on their part. That would be nearly politically impossible to do so, yet it is a worst-case scenario that gives the people a quick way out of a law that was passed that proved to not work or it was unpopular. The people deserve a contingency plan in the event that they desperately want a law they passed to be done away with. Some temporary majority could pass a law that proved disastrous for the country and may be riddled with unintended consequences. This would not be a way for the Congress, the President, and the status quo powers in Washington to keep their power over the country. For an overwhelmingly popular law to pass and be overruled by the Congress would cause the members who voted to overturn the law political trouble. They could lose their primary or their general election campaign for re-election against another candidate that favored the law. It would be an especially difficult vote for the Representative or Senator to make if a majority of their constituents were in favor of the law. If any member of the House or Senate voted to overturn the will of the people, when a majority of those in their state or district voted for the law they would be in political trouble. This would turn up the heat metaphorically speaking on those in Congress to do what the people wanted.

To give the US Supreme Court the power to overturn the people's will is to protect the Constitution. The people could not vote to create a dictatorship or bring back slavery. This guarantees the supremacy of the Constitution along with the right to challenge a law passed by other groups that deem a law passed as unconstitutional. Even though we would have a direct democracy, the people could not vote to get rid of the Bill of Rights or the Thirteenth amendment. The Supreme Court would have the ability to ensure that the Constitution continues to be the ultimate decider in the country. There are plenty of things that the people could vote into law but one of those things is not getting rid of parts of the Constitution. Amending the Constitution would have to go through the traditional process. Since there would be ways to get rid of laws that were passed it would make the system work better. It would be able to handle most any potential problem that could happen in the future. Most laws passed would stay on the books, there wouldn't be ways to get rid of laws just so the powerful can continue to be in charge while the people see no change. The people will have so much power to change things in the country by having a direct democracy. There are many things that attract broad support that never get done. The people would not have to tolerate the polarized gridlock situation where nothing gets done at all.

There are some possible problems that could come along with a direct democracy. One of them would be if the American people voted to give themselves infinite money from the federal government. The people could decide to vote themselves infinite money from corporations, the rich or any other group in society. The people would only be allowed to pass laws that were constitutional. Any law that managed to pass that caused unbelievable redistribution would be met with a serious court challenge. If you look at states that have a direct democracy these kind of laws have not passed or have not been able to qualify for the ballot. The people would not be able to vote themselves land or to force the federal government to confiscate private property. The American people would support legislation that made America better and that benefitted the US economy. They can be trusted to pass laws that they feel are in the countries best interest. For the most part the people don't elect politicians that offer to take other peoples property, so in a direct democracy they are not likely to pass any extreme or unconstitutional laws.

Some feel that the American people could not be trusted to have a direct democracy. They may vote in a series of laws that hurt the country or undermine the Constitution. Maybe they would vote in ridiculous laws that would outlaw vaccinations or give dogs equal rights to people. There are plenty of people who don't trust the impulses of the American people. A temporary majority might favor a controversial law but that support quickly fades and the people are unhappy with the law and its consequences. A majority of the people are sure to vote in favor of something controversial eventually. The people couldn't pass laws that were unconstitutional and laws that were controversial would invite a legal challenge. The Congress could even vote to overturn a law under the right circumstances. The people can be trusted to vote on laws and decide the fate and direction their country takes. Most voters are so called "regular Americans" that support common sense solutions to their problems. They would tend to shun controversial ideas and gravitate toward consensus. Most people favor some kind of limits on what the federal government can do. They would be skeptical about giving the federal government too much power over certain issues. The more off the wall ideas would never usually receive the support that they need to be on the federal ballot. If they got onto the federal ballot they would more than likely lose in the general election. Ultimately a democracy is about majority rules and if the majority of the American people vote for something then it will become law. The results of the election would be much more decisive than a Supreme Court ruling or a Presidential signature. Most people would respect the principle that majority rules.

Wouldn't a direct democracy cause more problems than it would solve? There will be a lot of wedge issues to vote on and plenty of laws that will be polarizing. Wouldn't it aggravate the polarizing environment and make for more divisive politics in America? These are reasonable concerns but the current situation allows those intense feelings to fester. Politicians take advantage of the wedge issues to motivate their base to go out and vote. If they can convince their base that if the other side wins that abortion will be illegal or there will be no gay marriage again then they can motivate their base to show up and vote. The polarizing issues are already used to maximize voter turnout by scaring as many people as possible to show up and vote. The idea that everything that they care about and that their very lives are at stake are powerful forces that politicians use to get people to show up to vote. Nothing motivates people like fear. This solves no issue or problem and only allows a politician to get elected. Everything stays the same and the politician has power while the activists and passionate supporters are pawns in the politicians quest for a job. A direct democracy would put a stop to this situation. The wedge issues are trotted out every election for the politicians benefit and there is no resolution to any of these issues. A direct democracy would allow the people to decide on these issues and have some hope of moving on from these wedge issues eventually. After so many times that a majority of the people vote in favor of gay marriage or marijuana being legal then the opposition will eventually lose interest or give up. The issue will be more or less settled depending on the attitudes of the people. A direct democracy means the politicians; political parties and special interests are no longer able to use the wedge issues to manipulate the electorate. The people will be able to decide wedge issues so that the public can move on to other problems rather than continue to joust over the same wedge issues forever. This would reduce partisanship and would allow some outlet for the peoples frustration. It would be less about politicians and personalities instead it would be about the issues.

The next possible problem with a direct democracy is that maybe the people go too far. Maybe the people make a lot of changes and pass a lot of laws that make the country worse or cause lots of unintended consequences. The devil always turns up in the details of anything. These are some potential problems with a direct democracy. That's why there is a mechanism in place for getting rid of unpopular laws. The people could vote to overturn a law in the next election, someone could take the federal government to court and sue over the law, or they could solicit the Congress to vote to overturn the law. These contingencies exist as a correcting mechanism to help prevent unpopular outcomes from occurring. These are not methods that could be used to prevent the people from making any changes or to stop them from making changes that threaten the government or powerful too much. Under the current system unpopular laws can never be repealed, it is passed and then the people have no way of getting rid of an unpopular law. One political party has Congress and then the other and each side passes lots of laws that never receive any scrutiny again. The people have all sorts of opinions about a whole variety of issues and federal laws that differ significantly with the federal government. Government agencies, departments, and most of the federal bureaucracy are permanently off limits. The people can't get rid of any part of government that they don't like or view as unnecessary. The federal bureaucracy keeps getting larger over time and taxes have to go up to pay for it. Deficits and the national debt skyrocket while the people have no way of influencing the process much less controlling the process. With a direct democracy the people would be able to reign in the federal government and have the kind of government that most people have always wanted.

Another potential issue of a direct democracy would be if the people passed contradictory laws. Maybe they passed a law that required the federal government to balance their budget every year and they passed a large tax cut at the same time. That may force the Congress to make draconian cuts to Social security, Medicare and the military in order to carry out the will of the electorate. That's a conceivable scenario where there could be conflicting objectives. Yet the people should get to decide what kind of a government that they want to have. They are aware of the implications of most of the laws that they would pass. They would want to force the Congress to carry out their wishes and make the tough decisions that they needed to in order do so. If the American people didn't like the cuts or the consequences of the laws that they passed, they would be able to overturn those laws in a future election. There is also the possibility that the Congress could vote to overturn an unpopular or unworkable law. The Congress would only be able to do so if they had the support of their constituents. They would not be able to prevent the people from getting their way. In the beginning there may be some problems with contradictory laws but overtime the laws would get worked out and the people would put the series of laws and reforms in place that they wanted. Unlike the gridlocked Congress, the American people would be able to pass tough reforms that would be to the peoples liking.

What if there is a tie? Is there any mechanism in place that would decide the outcome in the event of a tie? That is an unlikely situation that each side would receive exactly the same number of votes. If it did happen it could go to the House of Representatives in order to break the tie and what the majority of the House members voted for would become the law. The law would not need approval from the Senate and President. It may not be an ideal scenario but there has to be some way of breaking a tie. If it went to the Supreme Court that would be a less democratic scenario, it may go to the Supreme Court if there is some kind of a constitutional issue at stake. Otherwise the House of Representatives is the only place it could go to. It's a body representing the American people and is the only one that does so based off of population. It would do the best job of reflecting what the people wanted as opposed to the Senate. This scenario will never happen more than likely so its not a very important issue anyway, but this would be some way of deciding a tie vote.

Isn't a potential problem of a direct democracy is that it is insufficient? All problems or possible laws are not always yes or no situations. There may be more nuanced options that people may need in order to make a right decision. This is a legitimate concern that all problems are not binary and that people deserve more options available than yes or no. In that case there could be ballot measures that would give voters multiple options. There may be several different proposals before the voters at the same time and the voters could choose the best option or most preferred option. The option that received the highest number of votes would be able to become law. In those cases an actual majority of the vote would not be necessary to win. This option provides the voters to give more nuanced answers to possible laws then simply yes or no. There could be competing proposals for everything from healthcare reform, environmental laws, welfare reform, taxes, the budget, military spending or any other issue. Giving

45

voters multiple options allows the voters to have more power and will allow them to specify what things they want. The voters could be presented with multiple proposals, which would allow more dynamic answers, which would give the people more control over their government. The American people always prefer having more choices to having fewer choices. Multiple possible answers or proposals being presented as options would allow the people more creative answers. There are some issues that are black and white and would call for a yes or no vote. Most issues in the world are grey and therefore more options are needed so that voters can better address problems and have more satisfactory results.

The next potential problem with a direct democracy would be if the people passed laws that were bad for the country. There might be a law passed that hurts more people than it helps. Maybe the people make a mistake and vote for something that looks like a good idea at the time. A law that was bad for the country would end up harming most people. That kind of a law would become unpopular with the majority of the people that it was harming. The public would lose support for laws that they didn't think should have been passed, especially if they were causing a lot of unforeseen problems. If a particular law became so unpopular that the people didn't support it anymore they could vote to get rid of it in the next election. There is the possibility that the Congress could vote to overturn a law on the peoples behalf. There could also be a court challenge to an unpopular law. When the Congress passes a law that becomes unpopular it most often stays in effect anyway. The people have no way of getting rid of unpopular laws under the current system. A direct democracy provides a self-correcting mechanism that will prevent bad or unsavory laws from staying on the books and will get rid of government agencies or taxes that the people don't favor. The American people would be free to decide what they wanted in their federal government and to stop or get rid of what they didn't want.

There are many laws that could be passed that would benefit the people. One of the best features of a direct democracy is that it would unleash the unlimited creativity of the American people. Any person or group could propose a law. They would only need enough signatures of people who are US citizens of voting age. Once the number of signatures was collected, the proposed law would be on the ballot. The American people have a lot of great ideas that go nowhere because there is no way for those ideas to become law. The current system has a lot of built in opposition to change and powerful interests groups that are pursuing their own agendas. There are many ideas that people have that could improve the country. The Congress, President, and special interests get little done while they are constantly pursuing their own agendas. The people should not have to do depend on those in power to make the changes they want to see happen. The people should be allowed to propose and vote on laws themselves. It would allow the will of the majority to be carried out. The focus would return to the issues and attracting support for those issues. There would not be so much emphasis on the politicians, personalities, political parties and the issues that are used to turn the public against each other. Things would not be perfect with a direct democracy; there would still be problems in the country. A direct democracy would be a way to make things better for the people, it would give the people a lot more power and it would allow the people to pass laws that they have always wanted passed. It would also be a way for divisive issues to finally get settled. Americans always say that they believe in democracy and that this is a democracy. Our system is not a democracy it's a republic. By bringing about a direct democracy we could finally call our country a democracy. Twenty-five states and Washington DC have popular referendum already. Traditionally the states are the great laboratories of democracy. If we bring popular referendum to the federal government the country has a lot of experience in administrating this system. In the next chapter I will discuss the idea of getting rid of the United States Senate. In order to make the country into a democracy there would need to be less power in Washington and the people would deserve greater representation than the states.

# Chapter Three

The next change that would make America into a democracy would be to get rid of the United States Senate. The Senate was originally created to give each state equal representation. It was the result of a compromise at the Constitutional Convention that resulted in a house of representatives, which is based off of population, and the Senate, which represents the states equally. The states needed equal representation in order to agree to join the United States. This is a dynamic that has changed and the American people deserve to be represented better than the states. The states have a lot of power that would not be done away with without the Senate. The Senate is not democratic and the people of the country are not served by having the institution. When you look at America it becomes clear that the Senate is not democratic, look at the contrast between the states of Wyoming and California. Wyoming is the least populated state in the country with around half a million people, California is the most populous state with over thirty five million people yet each state has two senators. A Senator from Wyoming represents around five hundred thousand people while a Senator from California represents around thirty-five million people. Does this level of representation seem fair? A persons degree of representation should not depend upon where they live. Giving each state two senators is fair to the states not to the American people.

The United States Senate has a tremendous amount of power. Senators are elected to six-year terms while the President only serves for four years. Why do Senators serve two years longer than the President? The Senators are able to run for re-election indefinitely, while the President is able to be President for only two four-year terms. Why is the Senator able to be in power forever while the President is only allowed to serve for two terms? There are plenty of Senators that have had their seats for thirty, forty, and over fifty years. This creates an aristocracy in the Congress. This is a group of very wealthy powerful politicians with a lot of influence. These Senators have a lot of special interests that they are working for as well. Over time these interests and the Senators themselves almost become one in the same. They are all on the same team politically and strategically speaking. Each side has a vested interest in the other not just staying around but furthering the others agenda. Being in the Senate is an elite club that is at the top of the social scene in Washington. It's a body that emphasizes the importance of respecting the established norms and protocols of Washington. They unite against any interloper who wants to challenge the status quo. It's an institution that is Washington and is against any change. The people should not be ruled by such an aristocratic organization.

The United States Senate was created during the Constitutional Convention in 1787. The Articles of Confederation, which was created in 1777, was a weak document that operated as a compact between the thirteen colonies. After the Revolutionary War ended in 1783, the new country had succeeded in liberating itself from Great Britain. It became clear in the mid 1780s that a new document was needed to replace the Articles of Confederation. George Washington gave his blessing to support a Constitutional Convention and representatives from twelve states plus Alexander Hamilton representing New York gathered to write a new constitution. James Madison was the main author of it and the representatives quarreled over the contents. Edmund Randolph of the Virginia delegation made a proposal for a bicameral legislature which became known as the Virginia plan. This plan resulted in the Connecticut Compromise, which was an agreement that large and small states reached that created the bicameral legislature. The lower house would have proportional representation while the upper house would be weighted equally between the states. The House of Representatives was based off of population and would be more responsive to the people with two-year terms. Senators would be less affected by the people and serve for six year terms. In theory that was done so the Senators would be free to pursue Americas national interests when they came into conflict with popular sentiment. The Founders wanted to emulate the British government (which they greatly admired) so the Senate was created to be similar to the House of Lords. The House of Representatives was created to be similar to the House of

Commons. The Founders wanted to create a new government that was largely based off of the British system, which they didn't think they could improve upon by much anyway. The Senate was also created to give equal representation to each state. Each state would receive two Senators that were to be selected by their state legislature. The apportionment scheme of the Senate was controversial at the Constitutional Convention. There were those such as James Madison who favored the Senate being based off of population. At the Constitutional convention each state had an equal vote and any issue could be brought up again if a state wanted. In the first round of voting the state delegations voted 6-5 in favor of proportional representation. Small states reopened the issue again later and that resulted in the majority of states voting for equal representation with a final vote of 5-4. Connecticut, North Carolina, Maryland, New Jersey and Delaware voted in favor of equal representation, their collective population was equal to around 1/3 of the countries population. Pennsylvania, Georgia, Virginia and South Carolina voted against equal representation for the states in the Senate. The collective population of those four states was equal to roughly 2/3 of the American population. If state delegations voted the same way that the representatives did, there would have been a 2/3 vote against equal representation for the states in the Senate and only 1/3 would have voted in favor. The Connecticut compromise was passed so small states would join the union and ratify the Constitution. The delegates at the Constitutional convention were also afraid that a disaffected state would join a foreign power instead of the United States.

The United States Senate was created in order to create the country and give equal representation to the states. Even most people at the Constitutional Convention in 1787 were against all states receiving the same number of Senators. This has created an undemocratic body of powerful Senators that look out for their own interests. These Senators that have been in office for decades secure powerful committee appointments and chairmanships. These committees determine what bills are even allowed to come up to a vote in the Senate. If a bill or proposed legislation cannot get out of committee it will not be able to get through the Congress and to the President. Being in charge of a committee gives the Senator more power in crafting exceptions and exemptions in the legislation for their friends and benefactors. All the while the average person with no influence in Congress has to follow the rules. Senators make exceptions for themselves and anyone else they receive substantial support from. Having a member in the Senate for decades is a large investment for special interest groups, political parties, corporations, and other organizations. It is also comfortable for interest groups because these Senators voting patterns are predictable and it becomes a very routine process. These organizations donate money to the Senators campaign, the Senator works on behalf of these organizations and corporations in Congress. These organizations and special interests most often trump the desires of the Senators own constituents.

Senators go to Washington to work on behalf of their own state. Not in the way that you would think. If there was a line of who was getting represented by the Senator, the senators own political agenda is first in line, second in line is their political party, and third in line are their desperate campaign contributors and financial backers. This ranges from corporations, to lobbyists, to special interest groups, to wealthy individuals with a great amount of money to donate to their Senate campaign. This can be quite a long line already. Behind all of these people and interests is the state that the Senator represents. It's not the constituents of the state that are at this place in the line, it is the state government that is. The Senator is constantly under pressure from the state government to bring money back home, to vote for or against legislation, and to fight for the overall interests of the state. This is not all bad, but it is another group of powerful people that are ahead of the people in line. Even though you would think the interests of the state and the people in the state would be the same, that's not always the case. The average person along with their interests and concerns are at the back of the line. Since each Senator belongs to a political party the members of that political party have to be happy. Which means the voters who are members of the political party in the state must be happy. For example, if you have a Republican Senator from Alaska most voters in the state are registered Republicans. They have to be happy with this particular Senator if they are going to vote for that Senator again. So that Senator

51

has to work to make these people happy. What about the other people in their state that are not Republicans? They are even further back in line in terms of who is getting represented by this Senator. The opposite happens in a state where most registered voters are Democrats. For the people that are a Democrat in a red state or a Republican in a blue state means you are the least represented entity in your state. Your level of representation should not depend on what political party you happen to belong to or the state that you happen to live in.

The members of the United States Senate are the most powerful people in the country but they are the least accountable to the people. They are able to remain in power regardless of whether they pursue the people's agenda or not. They are the legislative body in Washington that is captured by the special interests more than any other. Since the Senators are usually in office for decades and since most of them represent states that are either solidly Democrat or Republican they have little to fear from their constituents. These members of the Senate are permitted to make deals with corporations, special interests, lobbyists and others. These are the members of the Congress that have the least to worry about with respect to the voters. They usually get re-nominated by their party easily and only see the voters once every six years. This gives them a safe job and a lot of time in Washington, this allows members of Congress to be able to work for their own agenda while in office and claim that they towed the partisan line to those in their state, which most often is enough to get them re-elected. These are very powerful people who become quite wealthy through their office if they were not wealthy already before they were elected. These members of the Congress are the power brokers; a lot of them are on the bench to run for President or to be drafted to run for Vice President. Some of them are on the bench to become a cabinet member. Most of the Senators however do not want to give up such a powerful and lucrative position.

The United States Senate is the least democratic institution in the United States; each member representing each state is not democratic at all. All of the states are represented equally but this arrangement does not fairly represent the people in the country. The Senate slows down the process of passing legislation in the Congress and the members plus the system of the Senate make it difficult to pass legislation. The Senate was created to slow down the process of passing legislation where the House of Representatives was more populist. Senators can stop votes from taking place, powerful committee members can table legislation and individual members can filibuster for as long as they can. They are powerful people who can do a lot for people who have the money and connections to receive an audience with them. A Senator is in a position to grant favors and help advance or destroy legislation. This makes the United States Senate the most powerful body in Washington yet they are not directly responsible to the people, often times the Senate stands in the way of the peoples will. The American people deserve to not be ruled by the Senate. Often the House of Representatives will pass a law and the Senate will not, they are preventing the will of the majority from being carried out. The people should not be told what to do by anyone in government much less the Senate, the President is under more pressure to act in the national interest than the members of the Senate are.

There are one hundred members of the Senate, most Americans have trouble naming both Senators representing their own state much less all of the other Senators. This makes it easy for Senators to hide from public scrutiny. Since each state has two Senators this further deflects blame from senators. The people will be upset with the Senate in general, but they may look at their own states Senators favorably. This dynamic also makes the Senate powerful, the Senate is not exactly democratic, not only does each Senator from different states represent a different number of people each Senator also has the ability to stop things from happening in Congress. If we only had the House of Representatives we could get things through the Congress much faster. We would also have laws that had the support of the people. This is because the House of Representatives is based on population and we should increase the number of representatives in the House (which is left to a future chapter). The filibuster is a way that a Senator can prevent popular bills from even being voted on. Not to mention there is the difficulty in one party gaining majority control of the Senate. Even if a political party like the Democratic Party have a majority of the hundred seats in the Senate it is still difficult for them to pass anything. There would have to be sixty Democrat Senators for them to easily pass things through, this is because filibusters can't happen with sixty votes. It happens when one political party is popular and becomes powerful. When a party lacks at least sixty of the Senate seats it becomes a great deal more difficult for anything to get done, this was done by design the Founders did not believe in a federal government that did very much. The Senate was created to slow down action in the Congress. The House of Representatives since it is based on population was meant to reflect the will of the people more and the two houses of Congress would then pass bills and compromise. The states are more powerful in the Senate, while the people are more influential in the House of Representatives. This was created as a compromise between small and large states. Smaller states were afraid that they would not have much influence in a House of Representatives. The Senate was created to give each state an equal say which is why each state has two Senators each and the compromise was necessary for the 1787 Convention. It was created out of a compromise between the colonies with large populations like Virginia and New York and the colonies with small populations. The smaller colonies wanted equal representation in the new Congress with the more populated states. Having a House of Representatives and a Senate was that compromise. That dynamic is no longer necessary; the United States does not need a Senate in order to exist anymore. We could have a better situation where the government is built around the people. That would be a democracy and getting rid of the Senate would be a step in the process of making America into a democracy.

In our current system there are checks and balances. There is the legislative branch, the executive branch and the judicial branch. There are three branches of the federal government so one branch does not become too powerful. If one branch tries to become too powerful, the other two branches can stop it. This ensures in theory that no branch of the federal government is too powerful. The states also have power in checking the federal government. Where is the peoples check against the government? The Senate was designed to give the states a place at the table in Washington and to ensure that the states had a check against the federal government. This is why state legislatures selected their states Senators in the beginning. The system of government we have was designed to get little done and the Senate is a body that slows down the process of passing laws. The Senate is not democratic and the body does not reflect the peoples will. The House of Representatives alone would get things done much faster. It would allow the peoples will to be done much easier. It would greatly increase the productivity of the Congress. Gridlock would not be so much of a problem in the future if there were no Senate.

The Senate is made up of people who serve in Washington for decades. These are the most powerful politicians in the country. They serve the longest terms at six years each, while governors and presidents are elected to four-year terms, a lot of mayors are elected to four-year terms and members of the House of Representatives are elected to two-year terms. Most of the Senators come from states that are either solidly Republican or solidly Democrat. Which means it is very easy for a Republican Senator to continue to get re-elected indefinitely from a state that is Republican. It's also very easy for a Democrat Senator to keep getting re-elected from a state that tends to vote Democrat. There are far fewer senators that represent swing states and therefore face a regular risk of being a casualty of the constantly rising and declining fortunes of the Democrats and Republicans. This kind of political stability means that these politicians are increasingly disconnected from voters. The interests of special interest groups and the interests of their political party capture these senators. They work for these groups instead of working for their own constituents. Since most senators are in safe jobs that allows them more time to maneuver in Washington and become more ingrained in the culture. They become more interested with their lives in Washington and become comfortable and complacent. They have no realistic fear of losing their job so they lack incentive to do as well as they can for their constituents and their state. The average person is ignored in this current situation. They have no recourse for getting their senators attention much less getting them to do anything for them. Only Senators from the so-called swing states are under legitimate pressure to do what most voters in their state want. Yet this is limited given their political party and special interests influence. Even though there are maybe a dozen swing states and therefore around twenty-four senators who are in this position does not matter much because there are a far larger number of Senators that represent non-swing states. Since senators only have to go before the voters once every six years anyway most Senators don't have a care in the world.

Senators are free to exert their leverage in advancing their political careers further or pursuing pet projects of their own. Most senators are looking for a promotion and will try to use their position to get elected President. They will accept an invitation to be Vice President and they will settle for being a cabinet member in some cases. Usually most of them prefer to remain in the senate, it is the most powerful job that someone could have besides being President. Individual senators are arguably more powerful than the President because they have safe secure jobs and they will be in Washington for decades. While the President is under considerable scrutiny from all corners of American society and has term limits. The people also have control over the President by deciding if they will vote for them or not. The people have no direct control over the entire senate body the way that they do with the President and the executive branch. The senate is a far less responsive and accountable body to the American people than the President. They are not forced to act on behalf of those that they represent very often. More often than anything there is gridlock, the Senate is the half of the Congress where gridlock is a more severe problem. The Senate was created to slow down the process of passing legislation and was meant to stop anything too populist or radical from happening. Most of the special interests, corporations, lobbyists and other power brokers must approve for legislation to pass. In order to win that approval there are times that legislation has specific sections that deal with granting those powerful groups something that they want. It doesn't have to have anything at all to do with the legislation that is being passed. These are secret deals that make up the regular activity of creating and passing laws and legislation. If power brokers in Washington don't approve the Senators will at least give them enough to make it so they will not kill a bill or try to oppose legislation. Special interests are very powerful and have a way of getting senators to write legislation that benefits them specifically in order to earn their support or to prevent their opposition. This all slows down the process of creating legislation and this stops any kind of law from passing that special interests oppose. The senate is where this problem with representative government is most acute. The Senate is unable or unwilling to get anything done while the House of Representatives is acting more on behalf of the people, yet that depends on what political party currently has the majority in the house. The House of Representatives is hardly a perfect institution, yet it will at least reflect the will of the American people more effectively than the Senate. Senators are influenced by a large group of people and organizations. Senators that are in office for decades make some powerful friends and connections; they are also good at pleasing the interests groups of their political party and their state. Senators must please these groups or they risk losing their Senate seat, this requires a lot of time, effort and overtures to please these different groups. This becomes demanding work for Senators but the payoff is large, they can be in the Senate for decades. Sometimes there are Senators who die in office of old age because they have been in office for so long. These Senators would still be in the Senate right now if only they could live forever.

The Senate is slow to adopting legislation; the compromise legislation that takes place between the Senate and House of Representatives takes even more time. One bill will pass in the House and another bill will pass in the Senate. Often times these two bills have critical differences with each other that must be worked out. This process is called reconciliation and this has to be done in order to create legislation that will pass the House, the Senate and get the Presidents signature. Special interests and lobbyists are heavily involved in the legislative process from behind the scenes. This process dilutes the bill brought by the House; it makes the bill more amendable to the Senators political careers and it also makes the bill more amendable to the Senators political benefactors. This is the so-called sausage making process of creating legislation in Congress. It's always been part of the process of creating and passing legislation since the beginning and is how a republic functions. This process has less and less to do with the people as it goes through the Congress. Different interest groups, corporations, lobbyists and wealthy individuals put their imprint on the legislation that's gives them exemptions, exceptions and other specialized treatment that makes up the fine print on most pieces of legislation that we have to pass in order to find out what's in it. Getting rid of the Senate would reduce the problems that come with having a republic. The people are not well represented, special interests and politicians are too powerful and the process of creating legislation is murky. Getting rid of the Senate would be a vital part in turning America into a democracy, their very existence stands in the way of the American people.

The people deserve to have laws passed that they support. There are countless problems in the United States that receive no attention because of gridlock and the federal governments inability to solve the countries problems. The problems fester and get worse while the people lose faith in the government and the country in general. Americans work hard and deserve a federal government that is accountable to them. They deserve to have laws that they support passed faster than the current process allows. The United States has a lot of serious problems that are left unaddressed due to the gridlock that ensues in Washington. The Senate is the body that is the most responsible for that gridlock and the Senate does not reflect the will of the people very often. It is an institution that operates to slow down legislation. It is a break where the House of Representatives is an accelerator. Members of the Senate have little reason to pass popular legislation. Even if there were a member that decided to work on behalf of the people honestly, there would be at least ninety-nine others that would stand in their way. It's not that all the Senators are against doing anything good for the country, the institution causes them to better serve special interests and their private interests over the interests of the American people in general. It's a natural outcome of a republican form of government and America has always been this way. Americans have a rising appetite for more participation in the federal government and there is an ever-greater demand for democracy. Getting rid of the Senate would be a step in the process of making America into a democracy.

Senators are looking out for their political interests above anything else. The best politicians are the ones who make you forget that they are politicians. They are not the most concerned with passing popular legislation. The Senate prevents a lot of legislation from even coming to a vote. Senators have to run for re-election every six years and they have to raise millions of dollars to win an election. This requires them to constantly court interest groups and corporations who will give them money for their campaigns. This also requires members of the Senate to vote for legislation that benefits the campaign contributors and to vote against legislation that harms their campaign contributors. Since there are not average people inundating the Congress daily and demanding that things be done, those Senators are going to do something else. Behind closed doors they will do what their campaign contributors instruct them to do. The Senators must spend a lot of time courting special interest groups, lobbyists, corporations, their political party, and other individuals. Senators need money, connections, friends, and votes to get re-elected. This makes it difficult for Senators to act independently of these sources of influence. Senators who lack enough money, who disappoint important interests in their party, or who fail to vote along with their party run the risk of losing their seat. It's the most basic need of any politician to have a job and they will do whatever they have to in order to have one. Given all of the political realities for Senators, they can't possibly serve their constituents 100% of the time. Their most base political necessities will come into direct conflict with their campaign contributors if they tried to do that. Whereas a direct democracy would allow the average person to get to vote on issues, the public would be the best served under this alternative. The public would be able to serve itself 100% of the time every time they went to the polls.

Senators must spend a lot of time campaigning for re-election. Throughout their political lives they are always campaigning and raising money. During an election year when they are up for re-election this is about an entire year that they are not paying close attention to affairs in Washington. Especially the senators representing swing states are heavily involved with their campaigns. They are very concerned about staying in power, which is their first priority. There are plenty of organizations and people that influence Senators. Members of the House of Representatives have plenty of the same problems, but it is more acute in the Senate because it is easier to influence one hundred people rather than four hundred and thirty five members of the House. Representatives run for re-election every two years and it is more difficult to influence these members of the Congress. It is much easier for the political parties, special interests, corporations, and others to influence Senators. They are also more attractive to influence because they individually and collectively hold so much power. Presidents come and go but Senators stay around for decades, these are the real power brokers in Washington. For special interests to donate money to a senator is an investment that will payoff for decades. It represents a return on investment that cannot be beaten by giving money to any other politician. It makes the peoples influence rather limited in this body of the Congress; when special interest groups and politicians have more power the people have less power.

The Senate is made up of very ambitious politicians; most of them are looking to advance further up the political ladder. This usually means running for President or settling for being selected as a Vice-Presidential running mate. This political ambition is one of the largest motivations at work that keep Senators from representing the people. They possess an ambition to rise in the ranks politically speaking and this means they have to be loyal to their political party, that loyalty is only second to their own political ambitions. They have to tow the party line and participate in the partisan jousting of Washington. They have to be team players who aggressively pursue their parties interests and legislation. If they play ball they can stay in Washington for years, it is also essential for Senators that are looking for a way to advance their political careers. Senators are not going to settle for keeping their Senate seat, this means that they are looking out for their own careers above everything else, that is what most senators have to do to keep their jobs. Their Senate seats not only make them powerful, it also provides plenty of contacts and a lavish government pension. The wealthiest and most powerful people in America are constantly courting them; they receive plenty of benefits along with multimillion-dollar campaign contributions. Senators do not have the healthcare that the average person has, they have something much better. The Senators have a lavish set of benefits while the things that the people want are low on their agenda lists. Senators are members of an elite club that is at the top of Washington society.

Since most Senators are looking to advance their own political careers, this will keep them from voting for things that will anger certain interest groups. They cannot offend certain supporters, groups, and individuals who they need to stay in power, but they also need to advance their careers. If they "play ball" and help their interests and their party, they are more likely to advance up the political ladder. Not only do Senators want to please their supporters, they obviously don't want to anger them either. They risk losing campaign contributions if they do; they also risk losing the primary for their party's nomination. Senators have a lot to lose by upsetting their supporters and they have problems if they do not please their supporters. Everything from campaign contributions, to sweetheart deals, to other forms of political support are also in the mix. These are all influences, motivations and factors that make Senators less beholden to the people. A direct democracy would allow the American people to be served first. The status quo in the United States Senate means that politicians, political parties, corporations, special interests and all of the most powerful and connected people in America are served first and only. Senators personally have a great situation; this amounts to a lot to lose. Senators can keep playing this game and keep their seats for a lifetime. Why would they choose to rock the boat and disrupt this situation? What incentive do they have? They not only keep their senate seats for years, but they also have other perks from their myriad of supporters. While they receive this support, why sacrifice it? Just because a piece of legislation may be popular, it may be unpopular with their chief political and financial supporters. Why anger these vital groups to support legislation? Who wants to commit career suicide? What person who worked so hard to climb this high would decide to just self-destruct? Individual Senators cannot overcome these institutional problems of the Senate and of representative government in general. Doing away with the Senate and having a direct democracy would solve these problems. It's about time that the American people can have a say and decide issues. We can leave politics and the politicians to the House of Representatives.

Most Senators don't have much to worry about, if they keep their head down and please their supporters their constituents would re-elect them anyways. They can just do fine in the Senate and have an unremarkable career they can serve for decades living a good life in Washington. Senators will be praised for their years of service and this is without passing any popular legislation. So Senators have little reason to support popular legislation and much to lose by doing so in some cases. They have no reason to risk political suicide over voting or furthering popular legislation. Most Senators keep their job anyways by doing what they are told to do by their campaign contributors. Their largest campaign contributors have strings attached to the money that they give them. If Senators in any way go against these people that will cause them lots of problems, if they go too far it will cost them their seat. Why would they risk upsetting their supporters and lose their seat to advance a popular bill, especially if they would be re-elected anyway? It doesn't make sense does it? Even if a proposed piece of legislation was popular and it did not offend their core financial and political supporters why would a Senator take the risk in working hard to pass it anyway? They have nothing to lose either way. Pass the bill, they get re-elected, don't do anything and they get re-elected. The American public simply holds little to no leverage over Senators to make them pass laws that they want. Even if it poses no political risk for them to try to pass something, even then it is near impossible to get a Senator to do anything for his or her constituents.

Considering the political reality that senators deal with this leaves representing the people pretty low on their to do list. For the sake of argument, let's say that all Senators were going to represent the will of the people of their states at all times. It would still be difficult for things to get done; there are plenty of states that are so-called blue states and plenty of red states. These states would require that their senators voted the way that the majority of those in their state would. This would even mean a Democrat Senator elected from a red state and a Republican Senator elected from a blue state would have to vote the way that the majority of the people in their state would on every issue. This would require them to represent their constituents instead of their party. There are also a number of states that truly are purple states. Lets say that for the sake of argument that these members of the Senate vote with the Democratic Party on half of the issues and with the Republicans on the other half of the issues. This entire scenario would still make it difficult for one party to gain a filibuster proof majority so legislation could pass. This scenario is completely unrealistic in the first place but even if this exceptional scenario could ever happen the people would still be left out in the cold. The Senate would still fail to do what a majority of the American people wanted and they would still fail to be a democratic institution. It would still be an institution that failed to equally represent the people and get things done. They would still be heavily influenced and controlled by the power brokers in Washington.

There is the other problem that even if the Senate passed anything without a filibuster, they would still have to reconcile their bill with that in the House of Representatives. Since there are two houses of Congress not one, each body passes their own bill and then the leaders of each come together to craft a compromise that can pass with a majority of votes in each. This can be a difficult process even when the same political party controls the House and Senate. It can be an impossible process when one party has one house and the other party has the other. Not to mention the President can veto legislation that does not have a veto proof majority in both houses. It requires two thirds of the members of the House of Representatives and two thirds of the members of the Senate to vote in favor of legislation for it to pass against a presidential veto. Creating legislation that makes the House, Senate and President satisfied is quite difficult to do. In American history it has always been the easiest when the same party controlled the Congress and the Presidency. This is because the system requires broad consensus if anything is ever going to get done. The process of passing legislation requires consensus not just from the politicians but also from the special interest groups in Washington. Everybody has to get their piece in order for something to pass, which is why pieces of legislation are often tens of thousands of pages. There has to be carve outs, giveaways, exceptions and addendums to give to various special interests or campaign contributors. It would be easier for legislation to pass the Congress if there was no Senate. Only having a House of Representatives would allow things to be based on popular support as well. It would better reflect the will of the American people than the Senate. Lobbyists, corporations, political parties, the politicians themselves and others would be able to influence Congress. It would be less worthwhile for them to influence members of the House with a direct democracy (Chapter 2) and when the House had so many more members (Chapter 8) it would get to too expensive to influence enough of them. Adding members would also greatly reduce the return on investment that a group would receive by providing a lot of financial support to a congressman. That along with getting rid of the Senate would make it extremely difficult for special interests, corporations, lobbyists and the power brokers in Washington to continue controlling the federal government. For special interests it's more difficult to influence a body where there are so many more members and when they have to run for re-election every two years. Members of the House may need more money and support because of that but they are also under more scrutiny and pressure from their constituents. The House of Representatives would do a more effective job of representing the people without the Senate. Even if there were no Senate, the President would still have to sign things into law. The President would be able to veto legislation from the House of Representatives if they didn't agree or think it was the right law. It would require two thirds of the House to vote for legislation to prevent the President from being able to veto anything. That would remain as always. The President and the House would have to meet and make compromises.

If they could reconcile their differences than they could pass legislation. If legislation were able to attract two thirds of the members of the House, then it would be too popular for the President to veto. Even if the Senate were done away with it would retain this traditional feature of Washington.

There could be some potential problems with getting rid of the United States Senate. One of the problems would be that the states would be concerned that they would lose equal representation in Congress. States with a small population would lose out to states with the largest populations, which would have the most representatives in Congress. These are legitimate concerns that smaller states would not be represented fairly. In the beginning of our country the country had strong states and a weak federal government. Today the country has a strong federal government and weak states. The federalist tradition is on life support in the current system. It's only a matter of time before the federal government is totally dominant over all of the states (including all Americans). The unchecked expansion of the federal government will continue unabated until America degenerates into a corrupt fake republic like most republics around the world are or an outright tyranny. Making America into a democracy would allow the American people to be in charge and prevent this possible outcome. Getting rid of the Senate would be a critical step in making America into a democracy. If the people were in charge they would have the power to restore federalism forever in America. Inevitably the people would vote to take power and responsibilities away from the federal government and give it to the states. This would restore federalism by empowering the states to a more equal plane with the federal government. The states would be able to take their case to the people that they deserve a change in laws that would benefit them. Getting rid of the Senate along with other changes that would make America into a democracy would certainly take power out of Washington and the federal government. The people would gain the most power but the side effect of the people having more control would empower the states and reassert the federalist tradition in America. The people would never vote to hand all power and responsibilities to Washington. People would vote to bring power back to the states and localities. If the states were still unsatisfied, they would be able to propose an alternative that would permit them to maintain equal representation.

Another potential problem would be that special interests, lobbyists and other groups would lose influence in Washington. Some may worry that since some of these groups perform lobbying efforts on the peoples behalf, that the people would suffer by lacking an advocate for them. There are many different groups in American society that advocate on behalf of many different issues and causes. They may worry that without a Senate, it would be more difficult for those groups to pursue their agendas or to influence members of Congress. These concerns are understandable but getting rid of the Senate would not get rid of lobbyists and advocates of various causes. There would still be a House of Representatives where they could advocate on behalf of whatever cause or issue that they wanted to. Without a Senate it would be easier to pass legislation in Congress, because of this it could be easier for special interest groups and lobbyists who advocated for popular causes to get changes through. A direct democracy would reduce the influence of unpopular or unsavory lobbyists and enhance the influence of those that are advocating on the peoples behalf. Not to mention, in a democracy they would be able to take their case to the people. If they believe in the rightness of their cause they should welcome the opportunity to inform the American people and try to earn their support. They would have the opportunity to take their case before the voters and take the opportunity to inform the American public on what they are doing. They could use it to raise money, awareness and get more volunteers. In the status quo there is no equivalent situation where charitable causes and organizations can receive attention from the public. They get lost in the sea of lobbyists and advocates that are found on Capital Hill. Especially since they don't donate money to any politicians campaign they don't and will not receive any attention or favors from the Congressman. They also don't figure high in their list of party or political supporters either. Corporations benefit by the power that they pay the Congressman for. In a direct democracy the situation would be reversed, corporations would have to pay money to influence the American people rather than Congressman. While charitable causes and organizations would be able to take their case to the people and receive more power to accomplish their goals rather than being ignored by the power players in Washington. Charitable causes and organizations would benefit a lot by giving the American people a direct democracy.

The next potential problem could be that getting rid of the United States Senate would make the Congress too weak. It could upend the delicate balance between the legislative branch, the executive branch and the judicial branch. If that body were done away with the Congress would have less power and may be overwhelmed by the other branches. The Congress would still have the same power that the co-equal branches of the federal government do. The Congress would be able to perform its constitutional function and duty with just one house of Congress. They could confirm cabinet members, ratify treaties and create legislation. They would still have to compromise with the President in order to pass legislation. There would still be a House of Representatives that would perform the role of Congress; the House should have at least twice as many members as it does now (Chapter 8). If the number of representatives in the House was increased that would allow the Congress to have enough power to represent the people properly. Increasing representation in the House would further their ability to represent their constituents. This would allow them to perform their constitutional function better than they can now. Special interests would have less power to influence members than they can now with the Senate. The President and the federal judiciary would lose power as well if the other suggestions in this book were implemented. The changes would take power out of the federal government and give it to the American people.

Another possible problem would be that without a Senate who would confirm cabinet members, federal judges, and members of the Federal Reserve etc.? With respect to cabinet members the House of Representatives would be responsible for confirming them. The House of Representatives would also be responsible for confirming other people to various federal jobs. That would allow the people to have more control over who was going to serve in the Presidents cabinet. The Senate is not a democratic institution where the House would better reflect the peoples desires. Members of the House are just as qualified as those in the Senate to confirm nominees. The fact that they are based off of population arguably makes them more qualified to confirm the Presidents nominees than the Senate. That would allow the House to give the people more influence over other figures in the federal government. With respect to federal judges and the members of the Federal Reserve, those figures would be subjected to elections and term limits (Chapter Five and Chapter Six). The people would be able to decide who served in those institutions and the process would be open to anybody who wanted to run. This would mean that the Congress would no longer have to confirm those nominees. The President gets to nominate someone and the Senate gets to confirm him or her. Getting rid of the Senate would limit the power that the President and that the special interests have. The House would get to confirm candidates that the President nominated, but at least it would be from a body that better reflected the peoples interests and desires. The House would perform the function of confirming the Presidents nominees well. They would be able to vote against nominees that their constituents didn't support and they would have more influence on the Executive branch by forcing the President to nominate people that could get through the House. The Senate is an easier institution for the President to get their nominees confirmed.

Some may worry that legislation would be passed too quickly from the House of Representatives. That without the Senate being there to slow down the process of passing legislation, things would happen too quickly. Maybe laws are too populist and the people have too much influence on the legislative process. Yet that would be the idea. The American people deserve to have their chosen legislation get through the Congress and become law. The people deserve a way to get things through the Congress faster than the current process allows. These days it seems lucky that the Congress passes a budget, much less anything of consequence to the people's daily lives. Gridlock dominates the

Congress and the body is unable to deal with large issues and serious problems that the country faces. They fail to pass many laws or any measurable reform that the people want. Even popular bills that they manage to pass are stocked with carve outs, giveaways and exemptions to their campaign contributors and political supporters. Corporations and other wealthy Americans create secret side deals with Congressman so legislation of virtually any kind benefits them and the public never finds out about it. Americans are not looking to Washington to be told what to do; they are looking to tell Washington what to do. Part of what they want is a Congress that is responsive to their desires and that gets things done. The legislative process would be faster, yet that would not bring chaos. The House of Representatives would be able to pass legislation that was more directly influenced by the voting public. Since they would be the only house in Congress they would have to take into consideration that they were it. Sometimes for political reasons members of the House give legislation to the Senate so that they can take responsibility for stopping it. They may want to be on record for voting for something while taking comfort in knowing that the Senate will prevent it from becoming law. This political Kabuki Theatre would become a thing of the past with America becoming a democracy.

Another potential problem with getting rid of the Senate is that you would be getting rid of a lot of experienced politicians. They are perhaps the most experienced politicians in Washington because many of them have been there for decades. Whether it is with respect to foreign policy, guiding federal policy, navigating the legislative process or dealing with a whole variety of other issues, Senators have a lot of experience in dealing with these issues. Wouldn't it be a bad idea to get rid of so many experienced people? Would the American people and the country in general be better served if experts on a whole variety of issues were replaced with relatively inexperienced people? These are some legitimate concerns with respect to getting rid of the Senate. However, Congressman have plenty of advisors who are experts in a variety of fields. Nobody much less a Congressman can be an expert in every conceivable field. Congressman are far too busy to be informed on all aspects of legislation or policy so they need people to help them with all of those issues. In order to best address a problem and to best represent their constituents or their state they have plenty of advisors or sources of help that they can count on. Senators rely on their advisors and staff to inform them and tell them the things that they need to know. If there were just a House of Representatives you would have a much easier time of passing legislation so there would be no need for experienced legislators to sheppard legislation through. If term limits were adopted there would not be any politicians who could stay around so long anyway if there was still a Senate. There would be plenty of new people who would run for Congress that would bring expertise to a whole variety of issues that current Senators don't have. The experienced Senators would be free to run for a different position or to serve the public by helping newly elected Congressman get up to speed on national security, national policy and the process of passing legislation. In the end there are plenty of think tanks, advisors, professors and academics along with a variety of other experts who would be available to inform Congressman on different issues. The retired former Senators could become consultants or advisors to the current Senators. The people with so much advice and experience running the federal government would be able to help others navigate the waters of being a Congressman. Getting rid of the Senate would not mean that there would be no experienced people in Washington that could guide federal policy. Members of the House of Representatives in Washington would have no shortage of experts and advisors to inform them about all aspects of their jobs and of legislation.

By only having the House of Representatives you have a body that is more beholden to voters, is more democratic and with less powerful politicians. This will make things better for the voters. It will ensure that they are better represented and that their views are more likely to be respected. The Senate often stands in the way of legislation from getting through the Congress. If there were only the House of Representatives, legislation would be passed faster and with less influence by the powers that be in Washington. Since Senators have to please their political interests, their political party, special interests, their state, and other people and organizations, this leaves the people that they are representing low on their list of concerns. If they do not please the list of organizations and special interests they may lose their seat. Pleasing these groups means voting for certain legislation and working to get rid of other legislation. This leaves the concerns of the people without a constant advocate. There is no special interest group in the Senate pleading with them to pass popular legislation every day. There is not a group of concerned citizens demanding that the Senate pass popular legislation. Even if there were it would not compete with the political power and the financial resources of those who really control Senators. The agenda of the people is the least of concerns for those that are members of the Senate. The issues that poll well with a majority of the American people are not issues that the Senators typically care about. They will only vote for things if they have to and they will vote for things if their very careers are on the line.

The average person does not possess enough leverage to make Senators vote for things that they support. It is difficult to come up with reform that would make Senators more accountable to their constituents. The fact that people can vote for their own US Senator only came about around one hundred years ago during the progressive era, there have not been any reforms since then that have made Senators more accountable. Senators pay lip service to their constituents and to the American people but at the end of the day they are working for those who keep them in office. The Senators large political and financial supporters are their political lifelines; there are also plenty of wealthy individuals who give money to Senators who have their support. Members of the United States Senate are the closest thing this country has to an aristocracy, they are among the wealthiest and most politically powerful people in the United States. Most of them serve for decades at a time and have plenty of connections. This body of the Congress does not adequately represent the views of the people. This body is not democratic and does not have much reason to fight for what the people want. The Senate is made up of career politicians who fight for those who contribute the largest amount of money to their campaigns. They fight for their own careers and their own political parties. The wishes of the people are ignored at best; Senators play politics with our deepest beliefs at worst. In the next chapter I will go into why members of Congress should have term limits. Members of the Congress currently are allowed to run for re-election indefinitely. The President is subjected to two terms in office, if the President is the most powerful person in the world why is the President subjected to term limits while members of Congress are not?

# Chapter Four

The next piece of reform that would make America into a democracy would be if the politicians in the Congress were subjected to term limits. All members of the House of Representatives and the United States Senate are permitted to be in Congress indefinitely. As long as they keep getting re-elected they are allowed to keep serving in Congress. Members of the House of Representatives serve for two-year terms. This means that every two years they face the voters and run for re-election while members of the United States Senate serve for six-year terms. Most members of the Congress end up serving for multiple terms in office that can go on for decades, few members of the House of Representatives and few Senators serve for only a couple of terms. The longer members of Congress serve the more disconnected they become from their constituents and they end up serving special interests over their constituents. Congressmen get wealthier, more powerful and more attached to life in Washington the longer they are there. They become captured by special interests, lobbyists, corporations and other power brokers who use their wealth to control Congress. Term limits would reduce the power of the congressman and special interests while creating a Congress that is more responsive to the people. Term limits would give more people an opportunity to serve in Congress, it would create a body that was more responsive to the voters and it would constantly introduce new people to Washington. They will go to make a difference, serve their constituents and pursue other causes then they will go home. Being in Congress would be the culmination of a career instead of a career.

Before the Constitution there was something called the Articles of Confederation, which was the countries first constitution. Work began in July of 1776 after the Declaration of Independence and it was completed on November 15th 1777. All thirteen colonies ratified it and it was finalized on March 1st 1781. It was an agreement amongst the states to unify forever where there was less of a federal government and more of collection of sovereign states. The document stated, "The said States hereby severally enter into a firm league of friendship for their common defense, the security of their liberties, and their mutual and general welfare, binding themselves to assist each other, against all force offered to, or attacks made upon them, or any of them, on account of religion, sovereignty, trade, or any other pretense whatever." The only body of this federal government was the Continental Congress, which was a unicameral legislature or single house. The document established equal treatment and freedom of movement for the free inhabitants in each state, only the central government is allowed to conduct foreign policy, members of the Continental Congress are appointed by state legislatures, each state in the Continental Congress of the Confederation received one vote each, only Congress can declare war or peace, exchange ambassadors and sign treaties. The Articles of Confederation also stated that individuals may not serve more than three out of six years. This document called for term limits in the beginning of the countries history, whereas at the Constitutional convention they decided to not employ term limits. The proposal for term limits for members of Congress is hardly a radical or new idea.

After President Franklin Delano Roosevelt was elected to four terms as President, a Constitutional amendment (22nd Amendment) was passed to ensure that Presidents could only serve for two terms. Every President before Franklin Roosevelt respected the tradition and precedent that George Washington set by only serving as President for two terms. This was why there was no constitutional amendment barring Presidents from serving for more than two terms before Franklin Roosevelt. After this constitutional amendment passed, American Presidents were only allowed to be President for two terms. The public was concerned about a president being so popular that they would be able to keep running for re-election indefinitely. That would create a president for life, which would give the executive branch far too much power. Why aren't members of the Congress subjected to similar restrictions? They serve for decades and often serve for as long as they want to. Congressmen have more power without term limits and the people have a lot less power over Congress. With the American people having less power the Congressman have more power to personally profit from a career in

Congress. Since members of the Congress can serve for many years they make plenty of connections. Originally they may go to Washington to make a difference and help those in their district or state. As time goes on they want different things. They become more influenced by Washington and special interests; they become more interested in the ways of Washington than what is going on in the place that they represent. As members of the Congress reside in Washington longer, they seem to think it's their new home. Committee appointments are not only decided by what party holds a majority in the House or Senate, it is also about seniority. The longer a member of the House or Senate has been there, the higher their station in Congress. The senator that has been in office longer than the other senator from the same state is called the senior senator; the other senator is referred to as the junior senator. Members of the Congress that have been in power for decades secure powerful committee chairmanships. This gives them power and allows them to be high up in Washington society. This increased influence in Congress does not only come with a new title and additional political power, it also comes with larger dollar donations. Not all members of the Congress have equal power, the members of the Congress who possess important committee chairmanships possess more power to pass or stop legislation. Since these members yield so much power special interests have a lot of incentive to donate more money to these individuals to have sway in Congress. The more powerful Congressman are left to serve their largest campaign contributors during their decades in Congress. Having no term limits keeps these Congressmen in place and allows special interests to dominate. If we had term limits seniority would be a thing of the past and there would be new people coming to Congress all the time. This would make influencing members of Congress more difficult.

Members of the Congress should be subjected to term limits, most members are there for too long. Washington should not be about career politicians serving their own interests, it should be about what the people want. As people reside in Congress longer, they seem to forget what the people they are representing want. They lose touch with their constituents and become less familiar with what their people want and need. They become more interested in their own careers and life in Washington. If members of the Congress were only allowed to serve for a couple of terms it would refocus politicians back to pleasing their constituents. Senators and members of the House of Representatives should only be in Congress for so long. Members of the House should be there for four terms only. This would amount to eight years as a Congressman. Senators should only be allowed to serve for two terms. (This is saying that there still is a United States Senate). Why does the president serve for a four-year term and members of the Senate serve for six years? Members of the Senate should serve for four-year terms along with the President and governors. A six-year term is too long and it allows Senators too much time in Washington to do what they want while their constituents are not paying attention. A lot can happen in six years and it leaves senators with too much free time to do what they please. They should be forced to see voters more often than every six years. They forget about their constituents and become more and more apart of the Washington establishment. Pleasing their largest campaign contributors and their life in Washington is their biggest priority. Most Congressmen spend more time in the capital than in the state they represent. Often when you see an incumbent Congressman defeated for re-election they stay in Washington and become a lobbyist as opposed to going back home to the state they claim to love so much.

Term limits for members of the House would allow them to serve for a maximum of eight years. Term limits for members of the Senate would allow them to serve for a maximum of eight years. The Senators would be able to serve two four-year terms and possess more political power, which is what gives them a better situation over members in the House of Representatives. If the President who is the most powerful person in the country can only be there for eight years again, why not members of the Congress? When members of the Congress can serve for unlimited terms, they are able to stay in Washington for too long. If there were a higher level of rotation in Congress it would assure that more people served. It would bring in more people from a greater variety of backgrounds that would have the opportunity to make a contribution. With more people serving the public would always have someone in Congress that was in touch with their lives and aware of their problems. The people would be better represented by someone who was not looking to serve in Washington forever. Serving in Congress would be a temporary position where they could do goods things for the people and go home. With term limits it would limit the influence of special interest groups and the power of politicians. Term limits would assure that there was fresh blood in Washington. It would produce members of Congress that were more in touch with the people they represent. Constantly bringing in new people assures that there are eager motivated people arriving in Congress on a regular basis. The people would benefit by having a more interested member of Congress as opposed to the status quo. The members of the Congress who serve for decades work for their campaign contributors as opposed to the average constituent.

Term limits would allow more people to serve in Congress. If more people served there would be different ideas pushed forward. They would have more energy and a different perspective to give to various national problems. Most importantly term limits would give Congressman more of the American peoples ideas. That is because term limits would bring in new people to Congress on a regular basis. They would elect people that would carry out their ideas and policies. Different people have different ideas and there would be not just more diversity in the people serving in Congress if there were term limits. Members of the Congress that serve for decades get too comfortable and run out of new ideas. Most often they get different ideas as they serve longer, they begin to carry out special interests ideas as opposed to their constituents ideas. While new members would have new ideas to try to change Washington and make it work better for their constituents. New energy would be another advantage to having term limits. The new members of the Congress would have more vigor and interest. The Congress would be inundated with new people on a regular basis who were looking to challenge the special interests and the power brokers. The newly arrived person on Capital Hill would be more so than members of the Congress that have been there for decades. A lot of these congressmen are too comfortable, they have a nice job, they have been there for years and they are good at playing the Washington games. As the elections go by and they realize how secure their jobs are they pursue their life in Washington and make deals with special interests. They enjoy the perks of being a Congressman and the insider information that they are privy to. These are politicians that may be good at their jobs and do good things for their districts and states, but they have been in Washington for too long and have become out of touch. The benefits of becoming a Congressman are far too large and it enriches already wealthy individuals. If a public office is so sought after by so many the office obviously has too many perks and too much power. Members of Congress should have less generous compensation than they have now. If 18 year olds who enlist in the military are required to serve for four years and are given some money in exchange, members of Congress should have the same deal as service members. They shouldn't have a better compensation package and set of benefits than American soldiers. If members of Congress were paid the same as soldiers then they could say that they were serving the people with a straight face. People should not be able to use their seat in Congress to become personally wealthy. Serving in Congress should not be a job or a career; it should be a short-term stint in Washington that allows them the opportunity to serve their constituents. Once they have been given an opportunity they should be grateful and go back home and let somebody else have an opportunity to serve.

Representing people in Congress should be about representing people in Congress. That may sound redundant or obvious, but it obviously is not like that. It instead becomes about the politician, not about the people. When someone may defend the idea of a Congressman serving for decades who exactly is that good for? It's good for the Congressman. Why is the Congressman so important? Some would argue that a Congressman who has served for decades would have seniority and therefore would be better able to bring money and resources back home. If we had term limits there would be no Congressman there for decades to attain that kind of status. There would be no disadvantage to being a new person in Congress; everyone would be new to Capital Hill. Imagine the things that could happen. Congressmen that have been there for decades are more likely to be captured by special interests and lobbyists than someone who just arrived. Members of the Congress that have been there for decades have been receiving large amounts of money from corporations, special interests, lobbyists, wealthy individuals and other groups for years. This means that these groups have invested a lot of time and money into these politicians. This dynamic enhances the power that these groups have and it assures their various agendas are being served first. Constantly having new members of Congress and a high rate of turnover would make it much more difficult for special interests to influence or capture Congressman. If someone were only going to be there for a couple of years what would be the point of giving them so much money? They are going to be replaced quickly by somebody else that would make the investment a lot less worthwhile and decrease incentives to give to Congressman. Having a higher rate of turnover would also make it more difficult for special interests to control members of Congress. With term limits there would be a lot more Mr. Smiths going to Washington to shake things up as opposed to a pseudo aristocracy. If there were term limits these groups would not be able to have as much influence. Sure, these groups would still have a lot of influence and would give money to people in Congress. But if there are constantly new members in Congress, it makes it more difficult for these groups to cultivate a permanent relationship. It makes it less worthwhile for these groups to give members of Congress huge amounts of money (Term limits would work even better in conjunction with the other ideas in this book). The money and political support buys the politician, in exchange the politician serves those who give them the money and support. A special interest group would have a lot less of an incentive to shower a member of Congress with money and support because they are going to leave relatively soon. Term limits would make special interests have a more unreliable relationship with members of Congress. There could easily be new people elected that rejected them and their influence. Since members of Congress wouldn't be able to be there for very long they would be less interested in getting money from special interests. They wouldn't have a political career to worry about so they wouldn't need to make fundraising and grousing with special interests and wealthy donors a priority. The members of Congress would be more unencumbered to serve the people and wouldn't be a slave to their political ambitions and the people with the money to make it happen. Under the current system it's very worthwhile to invest resources in a member of Congress because that is an investment that will pay off over decades with most members. In the absence of term limits, it only benefits the politicians, special interests, corporations, political parties and lobbyists. The American people lose in the current situation, bringing in term limits would be a crucial step in making America into a democracy. Reining in Congress and all of those who influence it would be to the benefit of the people. Instead of all of that power being concentrated in Washington it would be concentrated in the peoples hands instead.

New people in Congress would more accurately represent the people in their district or state. When a new person is brought into Congress they have been in their home more recently than anyone serving in Congress. Either they have been serving in a local political position such as mayor or serving on the school board, maybe they have been serving as governor or attorney general at the state level and want to run for the Senate. These people are more in tune with people in their state. They are more in touch with local issues and local problems. They have a greater understanding of the average person in their state and what their people want from Washington. A member of Congress that has been serving for decades in Washington increasingly becomes detached and out of touch with the people they represent. They become more familiar with life in Washington and more familiar with partisan jousting. They become more interested in their life and careers in the Capital. Most members of the Congress have an easy time getting re-elected and serving in Congress for decades. That means that they don't have a lot of incentive to work for their constituents too much or to fight aggressively for the things they want and they will become comfortable and complacent in Washington. This frees them up to play partisan politics, work for their special interests and plot a move up the political ladder. The average person at home that they represent has no recourse to do anything about this. Congressman shouldn't be so free to pursue what they want; they should be forced to pursue what we want.

The people who serve in Congress should not serve forever. We should have a Congress made up of people who serve for a relatively short period of time. It should be about the people as opposed to having long careers for those that serve in Congress. There should be a larger mix of people who are in Congress. Term limits would bring in people with different ideas, different lives and different backgrounds. That would enrich the policies that Congress created and make sure that all segments of American society are considered and represented. There should not be the same old group of people who serve year after year, decade after decade. When these members can serve for such long terms they have freedom to serve other masters besides the very people they are supposed to represent. Their largest campaign contributors and their largest political supporters will dictate all legislation that they support and oppose. Most members of the Congress have no risk of losing re-election, this is because most members of Congress represent states or districts that are very Republican or very Democrat. Most of the members represent districts that have been gerrymandered into being very safe for the incumbent. That means that if a Republican member of the Congress is in a district like this, then most people who live in the Congressional district that they represent are Republican. The opposite happens when a Democrat Congressman represents a district that is made up of mostly Democrat voters. This makes these Congressmen safe when they are running for re-election and the same thing happens with Senators. Yet not exactly the same thing, most Senators represent states that are very Republican or Democrat. These are the red and blue states where one political party dominates the state. They have the governors mansion, majority of both houses of the state legislature, are a majority of their representatives in Congress and their US senators. Being a Democrat in Massachusetts or a Republican in Texas this is your situation and this makes their Senate seat very safe as well, they can do next to anything legal and continue to get re-elected. Considering that most states are very Republican or

Democrat most members of the House and especially most senators have this politically safe and secure situation. This situation gives most Senators and members of Congress far too much power. If you never had to worry about losing your job that would change the way you did things wouldn't it? Since most members of Congress don't have to worry about losing their jobs they are free to do what they please, or to do what their campaign contributors and political backers please. The politicians and those groups are all rowing in the same direction. For the member of Congress, advancing their backer's careers advances their career. For the campaign contributors, special interests, and other supporters, the politician advances their agenda in exchange for money and political support. This is a club that benefits all and no one in the club gets a free ride. God help those who are not members.

Members of Congress are also free to advance their political careers. This usually means making people in their political party happy above everyone else. Each party has many different supporters along with many different groups that support them. Only the politicians that make their party happy are the ones who advance up the political ladder. They have to do what their supporters want in order to stay in office, if they want a promotion they have to go above and beyond. They have to be as partisan and aggressive as they can be which best serves their supporters and campaign contributors. It incentivizes Congressman to be as political as they can be and to be as ostentatious as they can be about partisan jousting in Congress. This all contributes to the fierce political polarization and gridlock that is witnessed in Washington. A politician never gets the Democrat or Republican parties Presidential nomination by going against their party. A good politician is one that goes with their party, not against it. That means that members of Congress are constantly working for their party, special interest groups, their largest campaign supporters and others. The people that they are supposed to represent are actually at the bottom of the list of those that the member of Congress is seeking to please, much less work for. If you actually visit the capital you are treated as a hostile interloper rather than being welcomed by some Representative that's actually pleased to see a constituent. They just pay lip service to the average person when they are forced to make those awkward photo ops with average people when they are up for re-election. The politician is desperate to show that they are average people themselves who actually care about what is going on with other people rather than getting elected to office. They try to act as cool as they can to please the young people and have weird interviews with MTV to show that they are hip and with it. Try to find a member of Congress after they have won re-election, much less in other years it is nearly impossible to find them at that point in time. That's when most voters are not paying attention to that fact, but should be paying attention. We are the pawns of the members of Congress, they use us to get re-elected and to stay in power to pursue their real agendas. We are pawns in their game of staying in power for as long as possible. They are there to help themselves; they are not there to help us at all.

The American voters don't have a lot of choice; we can choose to vote for a Democrat or a Republican. Most of the time independent political candidates don't have much of a prayer in elections. The people are heavily restricted in their choices and lack any way of being able to do anything about it. For presidential elections American voter turnout was around fifty percent in the 1990's, it's been around sixty percent in presidential elections since 2004. Analysts and pundits bemoan the low voter turnout like it's the American voters fault that the political system doesn't work better. But American voters are disenchanted with the political process and rightly believe that their vote does not make a difference, because it actually doesn't in most races. A more democratic United States with term limits would make voters more interested in voting (If America adopted a direct democracy). Americans would feel like they were voting to make some kind of a difference rather than support the perpetual power of a politician. Only the Congressman is excited about winning an election, it makes little difference to anybody else. The voters would feel more interested in voting if it was about making decisions for the country and solving some of the countries problems. There would never be voter turnout approaching the Soviet level of 100%, nor should there be. It is called the right to vote, not the legal requirement to vote. Americans deserve the freedom to vote or to not vote, somebody isn't less of an American because they choose to not participate, after all America is a free society.

Members of Congress are there to serve their own political careers and they should not be permitted to serve in Congress indefinitely. In the absence of term limits they are able to reside in Washington without fear of losing their job. This gives the politicians and the Congress itself too much power. They have so much power and are so insulated from the voters that they are able to pursue their political career and work for their largest campaign contributors. The Congressmen have so much power that they ignore the demands of the American people. They should be forced to adhere to term limits; this would greatly check the power of Congressmen and the special interests. They would not be able to continue serving for decades while ignoring their people and being free to pursue their own political careers. With term limits each member of Congress whether they were in the House of Representatives or in the Senate could only serve for eight years. Then they would have to move on to another political job or do something else. After their terms were up they could run for the Senate, or they could go back home and use their vast experience to benefit their communities instead of themselves. There would be far less powerful members of Congress if they were only allowed to be there for a few years. Term limits would give the people and the states more equal representation by not rewarding seniority. The average person deserves multiple different representatives in Congress over the years instead of one that is sitting in a lawn chair for decades that claim to work hard on their behalf. If you took this power away from Congress and gave it to the American people the system would be more democratic and less corrupt. The people would be better served and the quality of government would increase. It would be a tangible step that the federal government could take to start earning the American peoples trust back.

Term limits would even take advantage of ambitious politicians and channel that energy into the peoples favor. Let's say for example that there is a new politician who gets elected to the House of

Representatives. She knows that she will only be able to be in the House for eight years. This means that she will be forced to think about a promotion after eight years or retirement. This motivation to perhaps get elected as a US Senator or to get elected as Governor in her home state means she will have to go above and beyond for her district. She will be forced to work harder, push more popular legislation and show people in her congressional district that she can get positive things done for them. That would mean that she would be less interested in serving special interests and the power brokers in Washington. There would have to be a visible effort on her part to show people in her state that she can effectively serve them too. This is if the Congresswoman wants a promotion by getting elected as a US Senator or Governor. If she were serving in Congress indefinitely, she may be an ambitious politician and try the above things. Yet she would not have nearly the urgency, if you know that you could comfortably serve as a Congresswoman for decades what's the rush? If she could be there for decades she would want to join the Washington establishment as opposed to fighting it. Being forced to do things for the public would also risk backlash from her political party and her campaign contributors. This would incentivize the Congresswoman to work for special interests and play the partisan games. It would be a disincentive to work for the people and challenge the status quo. The opposite situation would also work in the peoples favor. Let's say that the newly elected member of the House of Representatives is only interested in Washington. Let's say she pays lip service to voters but is really only interested in becoming a lobbyist after she serves in Congress. This could be brought to the attention of voters in her district and they may elect someone else who would better serve them. Term limits would guarantee that this member of the House of Representatives would only be in the Congress for a maximum of eight years. If the Congresswoman truly does a poor job, she won't be there forever. Even if she is unable to lose an election after eight years she will be replaced by someone else who may do a better job. She will be forced to leave after four terms and can go on to being a lobbyist and the people back home are better served by having somebody new who wants to serve and help them. Today members of the Congress can serve for decades and this kind of politician ends up poorly serving their constituents for decades under the current system.

To have term limits is to increase the likelihood that an average person represents those in their congressional district or state. In their absence it insolates career politicians. With term limits in place it would open up the process so anybody could run for office and get the opportunity to go to Washington to make a difference. The job would be less appealing if term limits existed and it would have the effect of making Congress more responsive to the people. If someone is only allowed to be in Congress for a maximum of eight years, it is more likely that someone will get into office that is really trying to serve those that they represent. This is because if you take away the lavish benefits and power that goes with being a Congressman, the job is a lot less appealing. If too many people want a job in government, it obviously pays too well. If the job is so lucrative and desired they should reduce the compensation and privileges associated with it. Term limits would mean that there is a greater degree of rotation among members in Congress and there are a greater variety of people who serve in Congress. This means that it is much more likely than under current circumstances that an average person will serve in Congress. Why is that a good thing? First of all an average person is more in touch with what the average person wants. Secondly the average person is not as interested in serving in Congress as a politician for life. Thirdly the average person is perhaps more interested in pursuing the interests of their constituents than someone who chooses to serve in Congress indefinitely. If being in Congress paid little and did not have many benefits it would not attract as many people. More ambitious career minded politicians would be more interested in a different job. An average person will be less likely to be captured by the special interests and lobbyists in Washington. With a higher number of average Americans getting elected to Congress there would be more Mr. Smith goes to Washington politicians as opposed to someone who wants desperately to become a part of Washington.

It is much more likely that someone serving in Congress will be there to serve their constituents if we have term limits. There would be new people coming into to Congress all of the time that bring in a new perspective. The higher the rate of turnover and the more people that serve in Congress the better. It will mean more people who want to make a contribution and have different ideas about making Washington work for their constituents. Politicians get too comfortable in Washington and they become captured by special interests. Most people that serve in Congress want a long political career; most members don't voluntarily leave Congress. Essentially all Congressmen are desperate to stay in office for as long as they possibly can. Most of them will do whatever they have to in order to keep their powerful, lucrative job. That means they have to do everything that their party and campaign contributors tell them to do. If they don't they will lose vital donations, support and they may even lose their primary against someone who those power brokers like more. Term limits will reduce the severity of this problem, when you have a greater number of people serving you are more likely to have someone in Congress that will work for the people that they represent. With the same people there for years it is less likely that someone will get elected who will dutifully serve their constituents. We should give more people a chance at getting elected to Congress. Term limits allows more people that chance. With more people who get to serve in Congress the people are better represented. They would have a Congressmen that wanted to make a difference for their constituents and go home. The current situation allows a person to serve indefinitely, which means that they become career politicians. This means that most members of Congress are looking out for their own careers over what is good for the people that they represent. Many members of Congress are able to serve for decades. They may or may not do a good job for their constituents, yet it's unfair that so few people get the opportunity to serve in Congress. You always hear the congressman say what an honor it is to serve their constituents. Why not give more people a chance at doing that honorable thing? The people deserve to be represented by different people ever so often. They are more likely to be motivated to work for their people more directly. This is because if they can only serve in Congress for a few years, they are going to be looking for their next job right away and they would be under greater pressure to please their constituents. This is better than the status quo that allows members of Congress to get too comfortable. When they are comfortable they do not have as much reason to fight hard for their constituents. They are much more likely to be influenced by special interests and the ways of Washington.

These are some questions that the average American should answer. Is the Congress about serving the people? Are they supposed to pass laws and legislation that benefit the people at home and the country in general? Is that why we have a Congress? Or is the Congress about serving the politicians and their campaign contributors? That is an easy question to answer for the average American. The Congress is there to work for us in theory. Term limits would change the relationship that the people have with their Congress. Most people are pretty unhappy with their current relationship with Congress. People want a change in the way that they are represented in Washington. They want things to get done and they want the politicians to work for them. They want special interests, corporations, lobbyists and other power brokers to have less control over Congress and national policy. They want a Congress that people feel like is actually listening to them and in touch with their lives and problems. The people would benefit by taking power away from career politicians and the power brokers in Washington. To give the members of Congress term limits is to remind them of whom they work for. It would be an important step in reigning in Congress and sending people there for a temporary basis that can work for them. They and their body of Congress do not exist just to fulfill a lifetime career on Capitol Hill for politicians, their body serves to work for the American people. The Congress is too powerful and protected from the voters; term limits would give an average American a chance to fight for the average person in Washington.

Members of Congress receive a large package of benefits that they receive for life. This includes a pension, superior healthcare than the people that they serve, along with a long list of other perks that come with the job. This is when most members who are elected to Congress are already wealthy in the first place. They receive only more wealth and power upon getting elected to Congress. This is part of the reason why there is so much competition for getting elected; the job has a lot more benefits and power than essentially any other job. Often you see people elected to Congress that don't have much money, yet somehow they become millionaires quickly after they are elected to office. They possess the connections and influence to legally amass a large fortune by doing things most of us would go to jail for. Members can go on to jobs that pay millions of dollars a year as a lobbyist or working on Wall Street after they leave office. During and after their stint in Congress getting elected is extremely lucrative and introduces them to many powerful friends and connections. They use these powerful people to amass larger campaign donations and in exchange they do more favors for these wealthy and powerful people. The average person in most of the country has no chance of getting any service from a member of Congress. The more famous members of Congress can also make millions of dollars by writing books and by commanding hundreds of thousands of dollars just to show up somewhere and give a speech. They demand a free hotel room in the presidential suite at a nice hotel while getting half a million dollars to speak in front of people. They either come expensive or they don't come at all. Getting elected to Congress is not just about power, it's also very lucrative for many of those who serve in Congress these days. Members of Congress regularly pass laws and carve out exemptions to the laws they pass. They create exemptions for special interests, campaign donors, corporations, and very often themselves too. Members of Congress live in a totally different universe than the people that they supposedly represent. Term limits would limit this madness by requiring that people can only serve for so long. The longer someone is in Congress the more powerful they become. This would prevent people from becoming extremely powerful by being able to be in Congress for decades. Bringing about term limits would mean less power for Congress; less power would mean less money for Congressmen.

Term limits would increase competition. Since people would only be allowed to serve in Congress for eight years there would be a large number of former members of Congress. After serving for only eight years in the House of Representatives, the average politician would not be satisfied with going home. They would want another office to run for and win. Over time there would be many former members of the House of Representatives or the Senate. This would create a lot of viable candidates to run for other offices and this would result in a great increase in competition amongst politicians. The pressure on politicians would increase and make it more difficult for them to ignore the voters and be captured by special interests. Instead of having a safe comfortable job that they can relax in for decades, they would have an extremely competitive situation that wouldn't last long. They would all be under tremendous pressure to please their voters or they would get out competed by another politician who did a better job at that. The people would benefit by making politicians work harder to get elected and get the political office they want. Making it more difficult to get elected will result in a higher quality of politician that gets elected. There needs to be more pressure on politicians to serve the people and do what is good for the country. The voters are better served by having more choices and more attention from the politicians. The average person does not seem to mind making politicians work harder for them, the average person doesn't want to make it any easier than it already is for politicians. There is intense demand for a responsive productive Congress that addresses problems that no other body can. Increased competition will incentivize politicians to serve the voters better and to take the voters priorities seriously. People benefit and get better service from more competition in the marketplace, the people would also benefit if this feature were brought into Congress. The special interests, corporations, political parties and lobbyists have too much control over members of Congress, anything that reduces their power and gives the people more would be for the better.

There would be some potential problems with having term limits in place. One of the potential problems would be that with term limits we would not have any experienced politicians. If people have to leave all the time how would any member know what they were doing? Wouldn't the country

suffer by lacking experienced people in Congress? Aren't the people better served by having

Congressmen with experience and who can do a better job of delivering for their constituents?

Congressmen would not be able to serve longer than eight years, this would not allow anybody to serve

in Washington for very long. Some may worry that the people and their interests may suffer from a lack

of expertise. Term limits would prevent anybody from serving in Congress for too long. Term limits

would not mean that there were no qualified people to serve in Congress. There would be plenty of

people elected that would serve their constituents and the country well. With term limits someone could

get elected to four terms in the House, which would be eight years. That is plenty of time to get up to

speed with the requirements and responsibilities of the job. Most anyone would get fired if they couldn't

figure out how to do their job in eight years, if they didn't know how they wouldn't last nearly that long

in the job anyway. If the Senate still existed then someone could get elected to two four-year terms in

the Senate. That would be a combined total of sixteen years in Washington for that popular politician.

That is certainly plenty of time for a politician to become quite familiar with the workings of Congress

and the process of creating legislation. Term limits would still allow people to be in Washington for a

number of years. They could get elected President after being in Congress for sixteen years, this would

be a potential of twenty-four years in Washington. In theory if someone were elected Vice President for

eight years on top of that they could be in Washington for thirty-two years. That is a very long time and

is consistent with how long most politicians currently serve in the capital. The people would be better

served with term limits than under the status quo. The American people don't need politicians with

decades of experience in Washington, they need people in Washington that work for them and are

responsive to their needs and concerns. There are plenty of advisors and experts that Congressman rely

on that help them make more informed decisions. Newly elected Congressman have plenty of help in

getting up to speed on national policy, creating and passing legislation and the ways of Washington.

People that are elected to Congress are typically qualified to perform their duties in Washington and term limits would only bring in new people on a regular basis. Term limits would bring new people to Congress on a regular basis that would be more in touch with their constituents. Term limits would allow the politicians in Washington to do a better job of representing their constituents and furthering their interests. Having term limits would reduce the power of special interests and that would allow the people to be better represented than they are today. Politicians spend years in Washington and they invariably become out of touch with their constituents. In a time consuming job that is thousands of miles away from home, it's understandable that after a couple of decades you are unfamiliar with the people back home. After years in Washington they end up getting closer with special interests and further away from those they represent.

Another potential problem would be if term limits were established people would lose the ability to keep a member of Congress that they liked. That person may have a high approval rating and may have done a lot of memorable things for the people at home and for the country. The people would not have the power to keep a member of Congress that they supported. Some may worry that it would not be as democratic to prevent people from being able to decide how long they want someone to serve in Congress. If people like a politician so much why shouldn't they get to keep them? If a politician were that popular they would be able to run for another office. There would be plenty of other people that would perform well for their constituents. A certain member of Congress may be popular within their district and they would be able to leverage that popularity to get themselves another elected position. If they wanted to serve the people so badly why can't they go back home and run for local office or work for a non-profit? The people would be free to elect whomever they wanted to any other political position. Term limits would benefit the people while it would prevent career politicians from serving in Congress for decades. If people liked a politician that much and the politician was all about serving the people they would have no problem moving on to serve their people in some other capacity. When in reality the politician wants to stay in the most powerful lucrative job that they can get. That lust for wealth and power is much more important to the politician than serving their constituents will ever be. Term limits would prevent these kind of people from being able to stay in Washington for decades and it would weaken special interests. While the Congress in general is extremely unpopular, many people like their member of Congress or their Senator. Establishing term limits would restrict the power of Congress and it would make them more responsive to the voters interests and desires. Term limits would take power away from the Congress and the special interests while special interests would have less control over the federal government. Term limits would weaken the hold that power brokers have over Congress and the people would finally be heard.

The next possible problem is that having a high rate of turnover in Congress would cause the people to be less represented. High turnover would constantly bring in new people that would not serve for very long. They may be less able to advocate on behalf of their district and constituents. Would the people and states suffer by having an unreliable group of representatives advocating for them? A high rate of turnover would not threaten the peoples interests or the states, it would actually allow the people to be better served than they are now. There would constantly be new people coming to Washington that were more in touch with the people. They would be more aware of problems and conditions back home. Since they would not be in Washington for very long it would incentivize them to get as much done as possible. Term limits wouldn't mean that Congressmen couldn't serve for long enough to be effective. Even with term limits a member of the House of Representatives would be able to serve for a maximum of eight years. Eight years is plenty of time in Washington for a member of Congress to make an important and lasting contribution to their district and country. Presidents have a maximum of eight years to accomplish things for the American people and most people feel that eight years is plenty of time in Washington. A member of Congress would have a sufficient amount of time and resources to serve the people and serve them well. After eight years they may become captured by special interests or be more interested with their lives in Washington. Term limits would incentivize members of

Congress to be as productive as possible. Not only would they realize that they would have a short shelf life, but they are also going to have to look for a new job after eight years. This would make them go above and beyond for those that they represent. Americans are used to being able to control and scrutinize nearly everything in their personal lives, what goods or services they want to use, online review sites are incredibly popular, consumers are becoming empowered and have rising expectations. They want and deserve a government and politicians that are more accountable and who work for the people above special interests. They deserve to have more control and more involvement with their government as well. Americans have an appetite for more decision-making and for a Congress that is responsive to their needs and resolving problems that affect their lives. Most Americans would agree that the Congress is out of touch and there are plenty of politicians who pay lip service to solving our problems but nobody who has actually succeeded at doing so.

An issue with bringing about term limits is that they are unprecedented. The Congress has never been subjected to term limits in the past, why should we do so in the future? Currently there are thirty-six states where governors have term limits and in fifteen states state legislatures have term limits. There is also the twenty-second amendment to the US Constitution that has provided term limits to the presidency. The states with term limits have been better served by imposing them. The politicians are more responsive to their constituents and it prevents career politicians from serving for decades. It gives more people an opportunity to serve and it makes it more difficult for special interests to control the government. Term limits with respect to the presidency has been very successful. It has resurrected the tradition and precedent that George Washington set by serving as President for two four-year terms. The Presidency is incredibly powerful and most presidents would never leave if they didn't have to. The country is better served by having term limits for the presidency and it creates more responsive presidents that are more determined to do good things for the country and the people. Since they know that they may only have four years or a maximum of eight years they need to get things done quickly. When you look at how much a President ages in eight years these days its all the more reason why term limits have been a good idea, it's a very stressful 24/7 job.

The next potential issue with term limits is that the people would lack leaders in Congress with experience. We have such a large federal government and bureaucracy that the people benefit by having representatives with more understanding and experience with it. With term limits somebody could be in the House for eight years and the Senate for eight years (If there still is a Senate) then that would be sixteen years in Washington. That would be plenty of time for a member of Congress to become familiar with the government and the various agencies. Members of Congress and especially senators have a large staff. Their staff is typically full of people who have a lot of knowledge and experience to impart about a variety of areas. There are plenty of knowledgeable people that would be able to assist the new members in understanding the government. That is assuming that they know nothing about the federal government and how it works when they get elected. The congressmen have advisors and staff that help them navigate the treacherous waters of Washington. The only people who benefit by not having term limits are special interests who capture politicians and the politicians themselves. There are plenty of knowledgeable people who would come to Washington and have the opportunity to make a contribution to the country that has given so much to them. If serving in Congress is such an honor then other people should have the opportunity too.

Another potential problem with term limits is that the states would lack representatives in Washington who were competent enough to adequately serve their interests. Since there would constantly be new people in Congress they might be less informed, less familiar with how creating legislation works and it might disadvantage them and their state. This is a reasonable concern but with term limits all members of the Congress would be new and less familiar with the process than a fifty-year veteran. All of the states and representatives would be on an equal playing field. At the moment the Congress is all about seniority, the longer somebody has been there regardless of party they are higher ranked than the newer members. That higher rank comes with more enviable committee appointments and gives them more power to bring money back to their state. That disenfranchises people who happen to have a new representative as opposed to other people who have one that has served for decades. That is an unfair system to the states and the American people. With term limits it would create an even playing field for all of the states and the American people in Congress. The other thing that is nice about term limits is that if somebody could only be in Congress for eight years (If there was no Senate), they wouldn't want to leave Washington so there would be a lot of experienced politicians hanging around who could help inform the new members about how things work. Those retired politicians would be able to inform the new representatives on the process, they would be well-paid consultants or advisors to the new members.

People deserve to have more power and influence in Washington. They should be the ones who get to decide who serves in Congress and for how long. People should be pandered to and served by those in Congress. Term limits would give more power and influence back to the people. It would give the people more control over matters in Washington. When politicians can only serve in Congress for so long, they will be looking for some other kind of political office when they have to leave. Whatever kind of political office they pursue when they leave, they have to have the support of those they represent. To make people happy at home will force members of Congress to listen to them and serve them. The people tend to support term limits for those in Congress and should get what they want. Under the current system the politicians and special interests get to crush the peoples will for change. The American people should get what they want and the power should ultimately rest in the peoples hands. After all, the Constitution begins with the words "We the people…" Members of the Congress should be subjected to term limits. We should not have to settle for career politicians who serve in Washington for decades. We should have members of Congress who are more responsive to our needs. A greater rotation of people in Washington would yield better results for the American people. It would also reduce the impact and power of the special interests that run Washington. In the next chapter I will discuss why we should have term limits for members of the Supreme Court as well as the other Federal courts. I will also talk about why members of the Supreme Court and Federal Courts should be elected, rather than be appointed by the President and then confirmed by the United States Senate.

# Chapter Five

Another step in the process of America becoming a democracy would be to reform the federal judicial system. The federal judiciary and the US Supreme Court have a lot of power and they are totally independent of the American voters. Federal judges are appointed by the President and then have to be confirmed by the United States Senate. That means that only the President can decide who can be a federal judge; the Senators merely have a veto power over unacceptable nominees. Once confirmed by the Senate, judges have no term limits and can serve forever. The idea behind this was to have an independent judiciary that was not affected by politics. In theory it is a good idea, yet in practice the federal judiciary is a branch of the federal government that the American people have the least control over. It's a branch that has been deeply affected by the partisan loyalties of the President. It's a branch that corporations, lobbyists and special interest groups have a surprisingly large amount of influence and control over. Anybody who wants to become a federal judge should have an opportunity to become one, the American people should get to decide who becomes a federal judge and federal judges should be subjected to term limits. Taking this power away from the federal judiciary, the President and the Congress would be a vital step in turning America into a democracy. This chapter will discuss these ideas and attempt to examine potential problems with them.

Article Three of the Constitution established the Supreme Court. It is the only court specifically created by the Constitution, Congress created all other courts. Section one requires the Supreme Court and allows inferior courts. There was not a set number of justices in the beginning, there were only four justices at the first meeting in 1789, now there are nine justices that include the Chief justice plus eight associate justices. Section two establishes original jurisdiction and appellate jurisdiction upon the Supreme Court along with establishing trial by jury, while section three defines treason and its punishment. Throughout American history the law has evolved and the court has made many rulings over the years. The history of the Congress and especially the President is widely known, yet the judicial history is not as well known. The first Chief Justice of the United States was John Jay and the courts first case was Van Staphorst v. Maryland in 1791 and the first recorded decision was West v. Barnes. One of the most famous Chief Justices in American history was John Marshall; he served from 1801 to 1835. In the case Marbury v. Madison (1803), Marshall ruled that the Supreme Court could overturn a law passed by Congress if it violated the Constitution; this established the precedent of judicial review. The Marshall court also ruled that the interstate commerce clause and the Necessary and Proper Clause granted the federal government more power. In Barron v. Baltimore (1833) the court ruled that the Bill of Rights restricted the federal government but did not apply to the states.

The next Chief Justice of the United States was Roger Taney, he served from 1836-1864. Taney had a more limited view of the federal governments power. The most famous case during his tenure was Dred Scott v. Sandford (1857), Dred Scott was a slave from Missouri who sued on the grounds that his master had taken him into Illinois and Wisconsin where slavery was illegal. Taney ruled that African Americans were not citizens and that they could never become citizens so he had no standing to file a lawsuit. He also ruled that the Missouri compromise passed in 1850 was unconstitutional. This extremely racist and controversial decision helped lead to the Civil War a couple of years later. From 1864 to 1873 Salmon P. Chase was the Chief Justice of the United States, Morrison Waite was Chief Justice from 1874-1888 and Melville Fuller was the Chief Justice from 1888 to 1910. One of the most significant Supreme Court decisions of the post civil war era was the Civil Rights Cases (1883); the court held that Congress could not prohibit racial discrimination by private individuals on the grounds of the fourteenth amendment. The other most famous case of the period was Plessy v. Ferguson

(1896); the court ruled that the equal protection clause did not prohibit racial segregation in public facilities as long as the facilities were equal. This is the infamous "separate but equal" case. These were landmark cases that helped institutionalize Jim Crowe and other discriminatory laws until the 1960s.

The Chief Justice of the Supreme Court from 1910 to 1921 was Edward Douglas White and from 1921 to 1930 was former President William Howard Taft. One of the most significant cases of the time was Adkins v. Childrens Hospital (1923) that eliminated a variety of state and federal laws to help workers. The Chief Justice of the United States from 1930 to 1941 was Charles Evans Hughes, from 1941 to 1946 the Chief Justice was Harlan Fiske Stone and from 1946 to 1953 the Chief Justice was Frederick Moore Vinson. During the Roosevelt administration there were many fights over the New Deal, which led to some of the programs being overturned by the Supreme Court. These were cases like Schechter Poultry Corp v. United States (1935), which overturned the National Industrial Recovery Act, and United States v. Butler (1936) overturned the Agricultural Adjustment Act. After these cases President Roosevelt proposed the Judiciary Reorganization Bill, which would have increased the size of the Supreme Court and would have allowed the President to appoint additional justices. This was President Roosevelts infamous court packing plan, which went nowhere and caused large loses in the 1938-midterm elections.

In 1953 President Eisenhower appointed Republican California Governor Earl Warren as Chief Justice of the United States, he served until 1969 and there were some high profile cases that occurred in his court. Perhaps the most famous was the Brown v. Board of Education (1954) case, this is when the court declared 9-0 that segregation in public schools was unconstitutional and overturned Plessy v. Ferguson. The court ruled in Mapp v. Ohio (1961) that illegally seized evidence could not be used in a trial. Miranda v. Arizona (1966) led the court to rule that the police must inform suspects of their rights before they were subjected to interrogation; these are the famous Miranda rights that people are told when they are being arrested by the police. From 1969 to 1986 the Chief Justice of the United States was Warren Burger, one of the most famous decisions of his court was Roe v. Wade (1973) which declared abortions a constitutionally protected right. The next famous case was United States v. Nixon (1974) when the court ruled that the courts have the final say in deciding constitutional questions and that no person (including the President) are above the law. William Rehnquist was the Chief Justice of the United States from 1986 to 2005 and one of the most controversial rulings made was in Bush v. Gore (2000) which ended election recounts in Florida. Since 2005 John Roberts has been the Chief Justice of the Supreme Court, Citizens United v. FEC (2009) and District of Columbia v. Heller (2008) have been larger controversial decisions that the court has made thus far. This has been a brief history of the major decisions that the Supreme Court has made over the years. The Supreme Court has made many rulings over the years that have affected virtually every part of society. The Supreme Court has been and remains a very powerful and influential part of the federal government. Supreme Court justices have a lot of power and have no accountability to the people.

Members of Federal Courts and the United States Supreme Court should have term limits. Members of these courts should also be elected to their position on the court. Once appointed judges can serve for the rest of their lives if they feel like it. They get appointed or confirmed by the Senate one time and then they are there permanently. A federal judge only goes before the Senate again if they are nominated for a higher court position. The public has been warned before about judicial tyranny, where judges have unchecked power. What happens at some localities and states is that judges are elected into their position, at least in the beginning. That does not happen with Federal courts or with the US Supreme Court. First, the President has to nominate someone to serve in a federal court or on the Supreme Court. Secondly, members of the United States Senate confirm the people nominated by the President to be judges. This happens when a majority of the Senators vote for that person to become a judge or justice. Members of the Supreme Court would have to run a national campaign, since they would be representing the highest court in the land for the entire United States, everyone would be able to vote for candidates running for the Supreme Court. Lower than the Supreme Court is the United States court of appeals. These are also referred to as the circuit courts or appellate courts. These courts serve different geographic regions of the country and there are eleven of these districts. There is another district that encompasses the District of Columbia and it is called The United States court of Appeals for the District of Columbia. This means that these courts only hear Federal cases that took place within their district. They are the courts that filter cases into the Supreme Court and then members of the Supreme Court decide which cases they are going to hear each year. There may be thousands of cases that are proposed but the Supreme Court may only hear on about one hundred of them. For Appellate and Circuit court judges, since these federal judges only represent a geographic region only the people who live in that region should vote for them. Those would be regional elections instead of a national election for the Supreme Court. They could be non-partisan elections which would attract potential judges. The people would get to decide who they felt was most qualified for the job and they would finally get to decide what kind of judicial philosophy that they wanted to see in a federal judge. Isn't it too much power for the President to get to pick all of the federal judges? Even if it were three different administrations that selected the federal judges, it would be only three people who would decide what the federal judiciary looked like. The Presidents install people that have no term limits and never have to leave. The public can't even remove someone who does a poor or objectionable job. This current system gives the President and the federal judiciary too much power. The President gets to make a large impact on the judiciary that is felt for years after they leave office while the federal judges have too much power. If the people get to decide who the President is and who gets to serve in Congress, why can't they decide who becomes a federal judge? Are the American people not capable of deciding? The federal judiciary is the one branch of the federal government that the people have no control over.

Members of the Supreme Court and the appeals courts would serve staggered terms, this means that all of the judges would not run in the same year. Since each judge would only be able to serve for four years, half of the judges would run in one year, half the judges would run another year. Since there would be term limits there would be many people that were not serving as a judge that would be campaigning to get elected to a Supreme Court position or running for a court of Appeals position. Term limits would result in bringing new people every election cycle into the process of running for a federal court position. After the United States courts of Appeals there are the United States district courts. There are ninety-four of these in federal judicial districts. Each state has a federal district court, along with territories like the Virgin Islands, the Northern Marianas and Guam. There is also a federal judicial district in the District of Columbia and Puerto Rico. Each of these states and territories would be able to elect someone as a federal judge for their state or territories United States district court. People running for the Supreme Court would be involved in a national election and people running for a US Court of Appeals position would run in a regional election encompassing several states. People running for a US District Court position would be running in a statewide or territory wide campaign.

For the other Federal courts like the US Court of Appeals for Veterans Claims, US Court of Appeals for the Armed Forces, US Court of Appeals for the Federal circuit, and US Foreign Intelligence Surveillance Court of Review, would not be subjected to elections. Since these are "special" courts that serve a specific purpose for Veterans, the Armed Forces, and Intelligence, the members of these courts should not be subjected to elections. Yet they should be subjected to term limits like all other federal judges. Judges of the US bankruptcy courts, US Court of Federal Claims, US Court of International Trade, and US Court of Private lands Claims, and the US Tax Court would also not be subjected to elections. However members would be subjected to term limits. If the people decided that they wanted judges in any or all of these courts to be subjected to elections, then they could decide to do so with direct democracy. (Discussed in Chapter Two) Even Americans get election or candidate fatigue eventually.

Federal judges and members of the Supreme Court are free to serve as long as they want to, most judges end up serving for decades. Once they become a federal judge they don't have to worry about being confirmed again by the Senate. This means that judges are left alone to serve for years almost regardless of how they do. Whether they make controversial rulings or very unpopular rulings the voters have no recourse whatsoever. For a body that decides something as important as what is constitutional and what is not, the people should have more control over such a powerful institution. A federal judge installed for decades of power shouldn't have sole control over deciding the constitutionality of various laws. They get to decide very contentious issues and this gives them too much power. The people should at least get to decide who serves on federal courts and have new people coming onto the federal courts on a regular basis. Another problem is that federal judges cannot be recalled or removed for misconduct either. If a judge or justice angers the American public they cant do anything about it, the judge will keep ruling with impunity. Judges should be subjected to term limits; they should not be permitted to serve for an indefinite period of time. It doesn't serve the people well by allowing them to serve so long. The position was not created to give judges a job for a lifetime; it was created to make an independent judiciary. Most judges serve honorably and do a good job. Yet they are disconnected from the people and should not be free to serve for too long. Members of federal courts should only be allowed to serve for two four-year terms in office, like the President does. Why is it that the President is confined to term limits and members of the courts are not? They can be extremely influential in the shaping and interpretation of laws in this country. The federal judiciary is so influential in American life that the people deserve more control over it. The people deserve to have a judiciary that they want and that keeps up with their lives.

Judges end up on the bench for years. Since they get appointed or confirmed by the United States Senate, they don't go through that process again unless for example they were a Circuit Court judge who got nominated by the President to serve on the Supreme Court. Most judges serve in their respective positions for years without ever being up for a vote again. Since this is the case, some judges have a tendency to make laws. There are two different schools of thought about being a judge. Some feel that the judge is supposed to uphold the law and go by what the Constitution says, others feel that the judge should attempt to proactively legislate from the bench. These conservative and liberal judicial philosophies come into conflict with one another throughout the US judicial system. Giving judges an unchecked amount of power gives the American people little to no ability to decide what kind of judge they want serving. Only judges that break the law or have serious violations end up being removed from the bench. It's quite rare that this ever happens and most judges go on to serve for years. Term limits would make it so judges could only serve for two terms of four years each. The maximum number of years that they could be on the bench is for eight years. This is for each judge position they hold. They could be an Appellate Court judge for eight years and then serve on the Supreme Court for eight years. In theory one person could be elected to a federal district court, appellate court and Supreme Court for eight years each. That would yield a combined total of twenty-four years that a person could serve as a federal judge even with term limits.

The reader may notice that there is a pattern with term limits. Whether they are the President, a member of the Senate, a member of the House, or a federal judge or Supreme Court justice, everyone gets to be there for only a maximum of eight years. The members of the House of Representatives have two-year terms, while everyone else has four-year terms. Judges that serve for only so long and who are elected are not permitted to wield nearly as much power as they have today and this power would go to the people. The American people should get to decide what kind of people they want serving on the federal courts and they should be able to decide what kind of judicial philosophy that they want federal judges to have. Federal judges should be accountable to the voters if they have to be accountable to anybody. Special interests and the power brokers in Washington should not continue to have a monopoly on the federal judiciary. By having judges with less power, this gives the people a much-needed check on the federal judicial system. This would let people decide who can and cant be a federal judge and the type of candidate would be up to them. The American people could finally decide what kind of judicial philosophy they want federal judges to have. Whether people are happy with the way things are or not, most would agree that they would like to elect members of the federal courts and especially the Supreme Court. Today, the President nominates these people and then the majority of the Senators have to vote in favor of the nominee. This situation leaves the average person with no way of influencing the process. Once the judge or justice is confirmed then they will go on to serve as long as they want to. The judicial system is closed to people that may be great judges but don't seem qualified to the Washington crowd or they don't share the ideological views of the President and members of the Senate. The power brokers and special interests hold an unwritten veto power over unacceptable nominees. There is a small elite club of people that could be nominated to serve on a federal court. Very few other people receive any attention from the President or one of the Presidents handlers. Term limits and electing judges would begin to open up this process and allow more people to serve on the Supreme Court and various federal courts.

Most judges are in power for too long, with decades on the bench they may become more experienced but they become more detached from the American public and what their interests are. Since most federal judges are from such an elite club in American society in the first place they are not that familiar with average Americans. Especially after they have been serving as a federal judge for decades they become particularly disconnected and isolated. Elections would bring in new people on a regular basis who were from a more middle class background and who were much more in touch with what the American people wanted. Federal judges see many different cases over the years, most cases that are seen by judges relate to crimes of varying kinds. Sometimes judges wade into political issues that some feel would be better to be left up to the people. For good or bad reasons some judges try to legislate from the bench. If they had term limits it would mitigate the amount of power that they had. If federal judges were subjected to elections then they would be accountable to the voters. The people deserve to have some kind of control over the Judiciary. Federal judges should have to take their case to the people, discuss their judicial philosophy and discuss their background and qualifications for serving. Current federal judges would be forced to take questions about various court cases and various majority or dissenting rulings. Today judges or potential judges only take questions during their confirmation hearing. With elections they would be forced to defend their decisions that they have made and discuss how they would rule in future situations. The American people would learn more about how our federal judicial system works and what is currently happening within it. That would benefit the public by having more information and being more informed about the consequential cases that the court is hearing or will hear. The court hears many different cases over the years that have large constitutional and social implications; elections would require the justices and federal judges to explain their dissenting or majority rulings. Elections would bring additional transparency and daylight to the federal judiciary. The federal judiciary is somewhat opaque to the American people, they don't really see it too often or hear much about their activities. Elections would ensure that the people received some kind of an update about the federal judiciary on a regular basis. If people want their judges to legislate from the bench then they can vote for people like that. If they want judges to uphold the current laws then they can vote for people like that. If the people wanted a judge or Supreme Court Justice that strictly applied the original US constitution then they could vote for candidates like that. Elections would give the people a way of deciding the direction that the judiciary takes and how involved they want the court in crafting national laws. Judges possess too much leeway in deciding cases and sometimes they make rulings that have a large impact on national policy. Judges should be allowed to make these kinds of rulings, but they may make decisions that are unpopular. The people should have some control over this part of the government; they should have some sort of recourse when justices and federal judges repeatedly make a lot of unpopular decisions. People forget how powerful the federal judicial system is in this country. It is a large part of the government that the people have no control over and some judges become arrogant over time. They become consumed with the power and prestige of their position and they will sequester themselves away from the rest of society to be uninfluenced in making rulings. They know that they can continue serving as a judge for as long as they want to and they know that they have no election to worry about and that they are not accountable to the people. This current situation gives federal judges immense power, elections and term limits would give a large share of that power to the American people.

Term limits would allow a higher number of people to serve as judges and this would improve the quality and diversity of judges. This higher level of turnover would bring in many people from many different backgrounds that otherwise would have had no opportunity to become a federal judge. Maybe they didn't attend an Ivy League law school or come from a privileged background, maybe they lack any connections in Washington. It's pretty difficult for most anybody to get the Presidents attention about anything much less consideration for the federal judiciary. This would not just improve the legal system; it would also be something that was fair to more people who would make great judges. There would be different people who would serve and over time this would bring in a high number of qualified people. The federal judiciary would be stacked with more people from the lower and middle classes and it would be a more transparent and fair process. The American people would get to decide what kind of people they want to serve as a federal judge.

Federal judges should be elected. Anyone should be able to run for a federal judge position and the people should be able to elect members of the federal judiciary. Only a small group of people are considered for federal court positions under the status quo. It's all up to the President who is even considered. That's too much power for the President that should be given to the people. Electing federal judges would allow the American people to finally have the ability to decide what kind of judicial system they want. At the moment, it's only up to the President, then it is up to the Senate to vote for whomever the President nominates. The Executive branch would lose power because the President would not be the only person who decides who can be nominated to federal courts. The Legislative branch would have less power because Senators would not be the only people who voted to confirm court nominees. The Judicial branch would lose power because the judges would be accountable to the people for the first time. This would make Washington less powerful and this power would go to the American people. If the American people could elect federal judges it would greatly open up the process. It would bring more transparency and scrutiny to the process. It would also increase the number of potential candidates. There is a relatively small list of people who could become a federal judge under the current system, they have to have the right kinds of qualifications and they have to have the attention of the President. They have to have the "correct" political views and judicial philosophy to get confirmed by the Senate. This disqualifies thousands of people who otherwise would be great judges. With elections virtually anyone could run to become a federal judge. If you meet the requirements to run for Congress, then you would meet the requirements for running for federal judge. If any person could run that would greatly open up the process to an average person. It could be a person that may not have the political ideology of the President or someone who may not have the pedigree of a traditional person who is nominated by the President and confirmed by the Senate. The variety of candidates would be stunning.

For the people to be able to elect federal judges it would greatly democratize a process that is very closed. Currently the President is the only person who can decide who is even up for a vote. This means that if for whatever reason the President does not like someone or thinks they are unqualified, they are not even able to go up for a vote. This gives the President too much influence on the

Judiciary, which is supposed to be a separate and coequal branch of the Executive branch completely. If the President is a Democrat, it is likely that they will nominate people to federal courts who share the views of the Democratic Party. If the President is a Republican, than it is likely that they will nominate people to federal courts who share the views of the Republican Party. There are plenty of litmus test issues like abortion, gay rights, views of the proper role of government among other things that qualify and disqualify a variety of candidates. After the President nominates someone, it is up to the Senators to decide if that person is up to the job. They can decide to not even vote for the nominee or they can vote to reject or confirm the nominee. The same litmus tests apply in the Senate as with the President. The fact that Senators get to decide who serves on federal courts gives the Legislative branch too much power. They should not be able to exercise so much control over the judicial branch of the Federal government. Electing judges would make the judiciary independent of the executive and legislative branches instead of being heavily influenced by those branches.

Electing federal judges would limit the influence of lobbyists, special interests, corporations, the wealthy and politicians. Since the President gets to decide who is going to be a federal judge, they won't select anybody that would offend their largest campaign contributors and political supporters. This gives these powerbrokers a tremendous amount of influence over deciding who becomes a federal judge. If you are a person that offends or challenges these groups, you have no chance of becoming a federal judge. The President will only select someone who will not challenge these financially and politically powerful people. Even if the President was someone who would, their nominee wouldn't last five minutes in the US Senate. All one hundred of those Senators have campaign contributors and political supporters. They won't vote to confirm anybody who challenges or offends those groups either. The President and the majority of Senators usually vote to confirm somebody who their largest campaign contributors and political supporters support. Those people will serve their interests while they are presiding in the federal judiciary for decades. This allows the corporations, special interests, politicians, lobbyists and other power brokers to heavily influence and control the US judicial system. Electing federal judges would free the judiciary of these influences. The American people would receive judges that would make rulings against the most powerful people in America instead of protecting them. The power to mold the federal judiciary would go to the American people instead of those powerful groups. Regular elections and term limits would prevent those judges from becoming out of touch and unaccountable to the voters. To elect members of the federal courts would cause a large change in society. It would take the decision of who gets to be a judge out of the hands of the Senators and the President and into the hands of the people. It would end the confirmation hearings and force judicial candidates to make their case to the American people directly. Potential judges would have to convince the American people that they are up for the job. Electing federal judges would give Americans unprecedented power and control over their government. The people should be permitted to decide who should be serving on Federal courts and the United States Supreme Court. This would unlock a great amount of power that is currently reserved for politicians in Washington.

Electing federal judges would make them accountable to the American people. At the moment federal judges are nominated by the President and have to be confirmed by the Senate. This means that the President would never nominate anybody who would anger their campaign contributors, political supporters, special interests, political party and corporate backers. Even if they would, a majority of US Senators would never do that. This effectively gives these special interest groups heavy influence over who can be a federal judge. If you cross these powerful people and groups you can never become a federal judge. If the United States adopted a direct democracy (Chapter 2) there would be many changes that would occur. The people would pass many laws that challenged the special interests, lobbyists, corporations, political parties, politicians and wealthy campaign contributors. After the people passed those laws, these powerful groups of people would sue and declare that these laws passed were unconstitutional. Since they have so much influence and control over the judiciary, they may be able to quash any change that threatens them in any way. They could stop many popularly backed laws with their continued control over the federal judiciary. They could stop America from becoming a true democracy and stop the American people from getting their way. If we can elect federal judges and subject them to term limits this gives the federal judiciary to the American people and takes it away from the powerful special interests in Washington. The people would be free to pass laws that actually challenged the powerful special interests and have a government that was finally accountable to them (Everything would be Constitutional obviously). It would be a vital step in turning the United States into a democracy by taking power out of Washington and giving it to the people.

Term limits would give people an opportunity to serve as a judge in the federal court system. Because judges can serve for so many years this creates few opportunities for other people to serve. There are a large number of eminently qualified people that would make great judges and would make a great contribution if only they were given the opportunity. Federal judges are of superb quality these days, they often serve for decades and are amongst the brightest legal minds in the country. The issue isn't that the current federal judges are not qualified, the issue is that the American people lack any way of influencing much less controlling the federal judiciary. Many of the current judges would strongly argue against elections. They feel that elections would compromise the independence of the legal system and would inevitably turn judges into politicians. The fact that they were turned into politicians would mean that they would have to raise money from special interests to finance a campaign and get elected. This political reality would harm the federal judiciary with unstable politician judges who would be strongly tempted to make political rulings that hadn't a shred of legal reasoning or precedent defending it. It would take away time when instead of campaigning for an election or raising money they could be serving as a federal judge or supreme court justice instead. How would a politician judge have nearly enough time to read and articulate a dissenting or majority opinion if they had to campaign? Wouldn't elections invite unqualified people to get elected who would serve poorly? Is putting the entire US legal system and perhaps the entire US political system in jeopardy for the sake of judicial reform a wise or necessary thing to do?

There may be potential problems with electing members of the federal courts. Some may wonder if the process is going to create politician judges who are more concerned with advancing their political careers than serving as a judge. Some may worry that judges become like other politicians who are influenced by special interests. The judges would be forced to spend a lot of their time campaigning for office when they could be serving as a judge. These are potential problems with having federal judges getting elected. Just because people had to campaign for federal judge wouldn't mean that they would act like politicians. Some of the people elected would be politicians but that doesn't mean that they would be bad judges. A politician is motivated to do as good a job as they can so that they can get a better job. If there were term limits they would realize that they would not be serving for long. If they wanted to get elected to some other court or some other political office after they would have to serve well. That would incentivize them to perform honorably so that they could have a good record to campaign on for their next political office that they seek. That would force elected justices to serve as honorable judges and align their responsibilities under the Constitution with the interests of the American people. If the voters were unhappy with how the judge performed they could elect somebody else four years later. The current situation is that judges are not accountable to the people at all. Elections would make them very accountable and would force them to discuss their judicial philosophy to the people directly. As bad as an extreme that politician judges could be, it would still be superior to the current dynamic where judges are not subjected to the voters scrutiny. At least those judges would have to take their case to the people, any person could run and they would be subjected to term limits. It wouldn't be a career; it may be the culmination of a career instead.

Some people may wonder whether Americans are responsible or trustworthy enough to elect federal judges. Some may worry that the American people are not competent enough to select somebody who would serve honorably. Wouldn't they elect unqualified people? Wouldn't they elect people who would ignore the Constitution? Wouldn't they elect politician judges who would destroy the American judicial system? The American people are eminently qualified to elect federal judges. If they can be trusted to elect members of Congress and the President why can't they be trusted to elect judges? There are judges subjected to elections throughout the United States, the people choose honorable people who serve the people and the law well. The American voters would demand that a federal judge act and serve honorably and in defense of the United States Constitution. For the most part they would elect people that were similar to the justices currently serving in the federal courts. Elections would require them to campaign and earn voters trust; this would attract politicians who wanted to climb up the ladder. That would not necessarily be a bad thing, those kind of judges would have a great incentive to serve as well as they can. Currently federal judges are free to serve as long as they want to. This means that some judges have too much power and do things that go against the public. The people have no way of recalling a federal judge or of doing anything about a federal judiciary that has a lot of power over them.

Forcing federal judges to get elected would bring plenty of people into the process that are focused solely on a political career. Maybe if they cannot get elected as a member of the Congress they will run for federal judge instead. Is this necessarily a bad thing? If judges were forced to get elected they would have to appeal to the voters. They would not have to make people happy in Washington. There are state judges throughout the country that are elected by the voters and their integrity isn't called into question. Electing those judges has not produced the negative outcomes that some may fear with electing federal judges. In order to get selected by the President and to be confirmed by the Senate, you cannot go against the special interests in Washington. Electing federal judges would allow people to become federal judges who could actually oppose the special interests and the power brokers in

Washington. There would be a large number of potential candidates running for judge that are far removed from the political establishment. If someone tried to run for Congress and they decide to run for judge instead, they have to make a strong case for why they are qualified serve. If the voters decide that the person is qualified to serve then that should be fine. The federal judge would be up for re-election four years later and would have to convince voters that they were serving well. If voters decided that the person was doing a poor job as a judge or would rather elect someone else then they could.

The next problem with electing judges is that they become too partisan. When you look at how partisan politicians are these days it is a reasonable concern that elected federal judges would be the same way. Yet many justices are already of a particular partisan bent given that they have to agree with the Presidents ideology to become nominated and share the views of most of the Senators in order to get confirmed. Elected justices would at least have to be open about what their views were and the people would be able to decide what partisan bent they want their justices to have. Federal judges have a partisan bent and are installed as a federal judge, then they get to serve for decades and there is no way for them to lose their position. That is basically putting a very partisan person into a position for life. The voters have no way of removing that kind of a federal judge. The partisan bent of the President is felt in the federal judiciary for decades after they leave office. If federal judges and Supreme Court justices were elected they would have to take their case to the people, be open about their judicial philosophy and political views. The people would be free to choose who they want serving as a federal judge or a Supreme Court justice. The American people may elect people that are actually less partisan than current judges. They would have far fewer litmus tests than the President and Senators do. Not to mention a vast majority of the American people favor a good judicial system that guarantees a fair trial, trial by jury and doing what is allowed under the constitution. They would not choose arsonists and other people that would cause trouble for the legal system and our country. Electing federal judges and Supreme Court justices would only cause trouble for the President, the Senate and the federal judges that are free to serve for as long as they like. It would also cause trouble for special interests, corporation, political parties, lobbyists and the wealthy who have a lot of power and control over the President and Senate which gives them control over the federal judiciary.

The next issue with electing federal judges is that it would dissuade the right people and attract the wrong people. There are some people who would perform well as a Supreme Court justice that would shun the opportunity because they aren't political and they don't want to be. There are others who would be a poor federal judge who are attracted to the position because they crave a political career and political power. This is a legitimate concern when such a large change to the judicial system is being proposed. At the moment becoming a federal judge is already a high profile and political thing to do. It requires being nominated by the President and being confirmed by the Senate. This is a political process that already dissuades private people from wanting to participate. The federal judiciary is also different than Congress or the White House; those bodies tend to attract ambitious politicians and people that desire a lot of power. The federal judiciary is different in that the people that want to become a federal judge are usually not politicians or people who desire future political office. They don't use the position on the Supreme Court as a stepping-stone to becoming President or Senator. Usually as with President William Howard Taft and California Governor Earl Warren it becomes the culmination of a career instead of being the beginning of something more. So far nobody has used their position as a federal judge to springboard into politics. If there were elections it would more than likely attract the same people that are currently attracted to becoming a federal judge. Ambitious politicians are unlikely to try to run for federal judge to get a better job, not to mention not all politicians have a background in law or as being a judge. If some random politician attempted to run for federal judge its likely that the people would refuse to vote for someone that they deemed unqualified. There would easily be qualified people on the ballot who would win most of the votes as opposed to unqualified people or somebody who obviously wants to move on to something better. The American people take their federal judicial system seriously and understand that there are grave constitutional issues to deal with. They want a quality judicial system that assures that the Constitution is adhered to and one that ensures justice.

A potential problem is that special interests will exert influence on judges if they have to run for office. The judges will be forced to raise money to run a national campaign. This would require millions of dollars and would be a very expensive thing to do. This would force judges to take money from anyone they can get it from to get elected. If they have no money, then they cannot get elected. This will give special interests influence over federal judges. This is already happening in Washington with judges serving on federal courts today. The President and members of the Senate receive millions of dollars every year from special interests. They are in the same bind that federal judges would be in if elected. The President and Senators will not vote for a Supreme Court nominee or a federal court nominee who would somehow anger their largest campaign donors. The effect of special interests is already happening and it would continue to happen if we elected members of the federal courts and the Supreme Court. The difference would be that the people would get to decide who gets to be a judge. The people are not bribed and beholden to special interests like politicians are. They would be free to vote for whomever they want. This is the opposite of what goes on today with the President and members of the Senate. These people receive millions of dollars from various special interests and they have to do what they want or they will not get the money. Electing members of the federal courts and the Supreme Court would also bring a lot of daylight to the process. The increased public attention, transparency and scrutiny would greatly expose the process. Electing members of the federal courts would actually decrease the influence of special interests.

Electing federal judges would mean that they would have to campaign. People are tired of political campaigns and commercials. These things can get annoying in the fall of an election year, especially if all federal judges were elected along with Congressman and the President. This may

117

seem like an excessive number of elections and candidates to vote for. In the grand scheme of things, it is a small price to pay so that we can elect people and vote. Federal judges wouldn't all be running every year; half of them would be running every two years. The staggered terms would reduce the number of people running in a given year, yet it would be more for the people to consider. The people should be able to elect federal judges. People may worry that federal judges would be campaigning instead of serving. That they may go to political fundraisers instead of showing up to judge a federal case. The Supreme Court is not in session all of the time throughout the year. Currently, each term of the court begins on the first Monday of October. The term usually goes on until June or July. This could be changed to accommodate an election that would be held in early November and allow Justices to campaign for several months. There could be a similar change that takes place for members of the lower federal courts to allow them to get re-elected. This is not an unprecedented idea. The members of the House of Representatives and of the Senate do the same thing. They are available to campaign for their re-elections easily while serving in Congress and committing to the responsibilities of both. Some may worry that campaigning would be unfair to members of the Supreme Court or the other federal courts. But if they don't want to take their case to the people then they shouldn't be a federal judge at all. They would be forced to tell voters how they would serve and what their judicial philosophy was. Federal judges should have to have the consent of the American people to serve in the first place.

Another potential problem with subjecting federal judges to elections and term limits would be that it would put the independence of the federal judiciary in jeopardy. How could federal judges be impartial when they were themselves politicians? Wouldn't they refrain from being independent judges and wouldn't that imperil the integrity of our legal system? Preserving the independence of our judiciary is very important. Subjecting our federal judges to elections and term limits would make them more independent of the President and of the Senate. In the current system only the President gets to decide who can be a federal judge and the Senate gets to approve or disapprove the nominee. This allows the executive branch and the legislative branch to have too much control over the judiciary. That compromises the federal judiciaries independence. Not to mention, there are plenty of special interests, corporations, lobbyists and other powerful groups that get to heavily influence who can be a federal judge. The President is never going to nominate someone and the Senate will never vote to confirm someone that would anger their largest political supporters and campaign contributors. That prevents our federal judiciary from being populated with people that would rule against these interests. Subjecting federal judges to elections and term limits would give the people the power to control the federal judiciary, instead of the President, Senate and special interests. The people can be trusted to select individuals who are worthy of being a federal judge. People would be free to examine their record and their rulings and choose whom they would prefer to serve in the federal judiciary. A vast majority of Americans want a fair and impartial legal system. Nobody says that electing the President and electing members of Congress compromises those institutions. Why shouldn't the people get to decide who can be a federal judge? Term limits and staggered terms would also help preserve judicial independence. Judges serving in their second term would not face the voters again so they would be free to make more independent rulings. Not all federal judges would be up for re-election at the same time that would help preserve judicial independence by shielding some federal judges from the voters. Those that only wanted to serve as a judge for a single term would help maintain judicial independence. They would be looking to be a federal judge for several years at the end of their career. Since it was the end of their career and they would not be career politicians they would be more willing to rule with integrity even if it means being unable to get reelected. These are factors that would help preserve judicial independence.

The next potential problem would be if we imposed term limits on federal judges, wouldn't that degrade the quality and experience of the people serving? Isn't the current system better where judges have decades of experience? That is a reasonable concern, but with term limits and elections judges would be able to serve for eight years in a federal court position. They would have two terms to serve which should be plenty of time for them to make a positive contribution. The other thing is that somebody would be able to serve for two terms in multiple different federal courts. They could serve for eight years as a federal judge, eight years as an Appellate court judge and then eight years on the Supreme Court. That would be a maximum of twenty-four years that they could serve as a federal judge. A judge that was popular would be able to serve for decades and that would permit the American people to have judges and justices with decades of experience. The people would still have experienced professionals on the bench and they would be able to select those that they wanted at the same time. The people would properly vet them and their judicial experience would increase over time.

Another objection to having term limits and electing judges is that legal experts feel that would compromise the integrity of the judicial system. Judges would become politicians and would collect money from campaign contributors in order to run campaigns. This would cause judges to become politicians who don't rule in the name of the law; they would do what their campaign contributors told them to do instead. These are some reasonable concerns that electing judges and imposing term limits could bring. However, a vital feature of our judicial system that allows it to be independent and impartial is trial by jury. There may be politician judges, but there would still be a jury made up of ordinary people. That would help preserve judicial independence, assure a fair trial and uphold all Americans constitutional rights whenever they step into a federal courtroom. Electing judges and imposing term limits does not eliminate the jury from federal cases. Not to mention there are twenty states that elect judges and subject them to retention elections. This has not resulted in a judiciary of dishonorable politician judges that make poor legal decisions. It has not resulted in the demise of those states legal systems or the constitutional rights of the people who live in those states. It has given the people who live in those states more control over their own government. It has given the people more control over a part of their government that is the least accountable to them.

People who serve on federal courts should be elected and they should be subjected to term limits. They should only be permitted to serve for two four-year terms for the position they hold. If someone were a judge on a US District Court for eight years, they would be allowed to run for the Court of Appeals or the Supreme Court. They just would not be permitted to stay in their current job for more than two four-year terms. Elections for federal judges would give the American people unprecedented influence and control over the judicial system. It would allow many people to be considered for a federal court position who currently have no chance of being nominated by the President and confirmed by the Senate. It would greatly increase transparency and bring daylight into the process of America selecting people to serve in federal courts. This would be from the US District court of your state all the way up to the US Supreme Court. The people deserve to choose who resides in these extremely powerful positions. This is power that should be taken away from the President and the Senate and given to the American people. It would take a lot of power away from the special interest groups and power brokers in Washington that have too much influence over the judicial system. In the next chapter The Federal Reserve will be discussed. Why we should be able to elect people to the Federal Reserve and why they should be subjected to term limits.

# Chapter Six

The next step in the process of making the United States into a democracy would be for the American people to control the Federal Reserve. The Federal Reserve or the Fed is not a very well understood institution but it wields an enormous amount of control over the US economy. The economy affects all Americans and all people have a stake in responsible Federal Reserve policy. The American people should get to decide who serves on the Federal Reserve Board and the regional Federal Reserve boards. The people that serve on those boards should be subjected to term limits as well. The Federal Reserve is essentially the fourth branch of the federal government. It is a body that is heavily influenced by Wall Street and private banks that get the Federal Reserve to pursue policies that benefit their own narrow private interests. Sometimes these private interests trump what is best for the American people and the US economy in general. The Federal Reserve should always pursue policies that benefit the American people. There has been a lot of controversy surrounding the Federal Reserve since the financial crisis in 2008. There are those that feel that we should get rid of the Federal Reserve, some want to audit the Fed and others want to reform the institution. Subjecting the Federal Reserve and the regional Federal Reserve boards to elections would be a sort of compromise between getting rid of the Fed and maintaining the status quo. The American people would decide who serves and those that served would have term limits. That would force potential Federal Reserve board members to take their case to the people and explain what the Federal Reserve actually does. This would benefit the average person to have more information on the Federal Reserve and what their policies were. It would require the Fed to communicate their policies in a way that the people could understand instead of the incomprehensible dialogue known as Fed Speak. Members of the Federal Reserve Board should be subjected to elections and term limits. Currently members of the Federal Reserve board are nominated by the President and then have to be confirmed by the United States Senate. The Federal Reserve has a tremendous amount of power in running the American economy. Everything from setting interest rates, to monetary policy to influencing the value of the dollar, the Federal Reserve has a lot of power over the economy. The average person has no control over who is in charge of the Federal Reserve and has no way of influencing it. For better or worse the Fed has been an independent central bank. It has existed for one hundred years without input from the people. This is a powerful part of the Federal government where the American people have no control and don't receive a lot of information.

The nations first central bank was called the Bank of North America. It was created by the continental congress at Alexander Hamilton's recommendation in 1781 and opened in 1782. This bank operated as a private business and when it first issued shares they became the United States first initial public offering or IPO. After the Constitutional Convention created the United States Constitution in 1787 the United States had an entirely new government than it did under the Articles of Confederation. Since the United States had a new government a new bank was needed. In 1791 as the nations first Treasury Secretary Alexander Hamilton's recommended the creation of a new central bank and Congress created the First Bank of the United States. It was given a twenty-year charter and it was located in Philadelphia, Pennsylvania. There were four reasons that Hamilton gave to create the bank. One was so the federal government could assume the revolutionary war debt of the thirteen colonies to establish a federal line of credit. Second was to pay off the war debts. Third was to raise money for the new government and the fourth reason was to establish a national bank and create a common currency. This bank was also a private company like the Bank of North America and sold shares to the public. Twenty percent of the shares were owned by the Federal Government and eighty percent were owned by private individuals. In 1811 when the banks charter had expired the Congress voted on whether to renew the charter. Vice President George Clinton broke the tie in the United States Senate and voted against renewing the charter. In 1816 the Congress created the Second Bank of the United States. That bank was given a twenty-year charter like the First Bank of the United States. Also like the first one it was a private company that sold shares to the public. Twenty percent of the shares were owned by the federal government and eighty percent of the shares were owned by private individuals. In 1836 the banks charter was not renewed by the Andrew Jackson administration, which fought a war against the bank and the banks president Nicholas Biddle. The bank operated as a private institution, which was liquidated in 1841, and the United States operated without a central bank. In 1863 Congress created the National Banking Act of 1863. This act created a system of national banks and the office of the Comptroller of the Currency was created to supervise the national banks. This act created a uniform national currency, this is when the US dollar or the greenback was created. Before this act each state had their own currency and each bank issued their own currency. With so many different currencies a uniform currency was needed. Finally this act was also created to finance the American Civil War. Many farmers had large deposits in national banks and during the planting season they would withdraw the money that they deposited in the bank. This would cause the national banks to run out of money which would cause bank runs. Bank runs would cause severe depressions and financial crises. The problem was that the national banks did not have a lender of last resort. They had no one they could borrow money from to give to customers making large withdrawals like the farmers. Bank runs happen because a bank only has around ten percent of deposits in the bank at any given time. The money that a bank has in its vaults is called reserves. A bank makes money by loaning out deposits to other businesses and individuals. When customers want to withdraw their money at the same time the bank would have no way of giving everyone their money back at the same time. The customers would realize that they might lose all of their money unless they go to the bank and withdraw it and this situation causes a panic or a bank run. Bank runs have happened as a result of as little as a rumor that the bank would go out of business. The bank goes out of business, customers lose their entire deposit or life savings and businesses and individuals cannot receive a loan. When this happens to many banks throughout the country at the same time it causes a financial crisis and economic depression. These occurred on a regular basis in the post civil war era. The nationally chartered banks lacked someone to lend them money when they did not have enough in reserves to meet withdrawal needs. This role or function is called being the lender of last resort. After the 1907 financial crisis occurred the federal government decided that they needed to create a central bank to help control the supply of money in the economy. Congress created the Federal Reserve Act, which created the Federal Reserve in 1913. It created a Central Bank in the United States that would conduct monetary policy. The Federal Reserve consists of a seven-member panel called the Board of Governors. They are given the responsibility of overseeing the twelve Federal Reserve banks in the country. They decide on monetary policy and supervise the banking system. Each member serves for a fourteen-year term on the board. Each member serves staggered terms, which means that one term begins every two years. One person gets put on in one year, two years later another person starts their fourteen year term and so on. The Board of Governors oversees the twelve Federal Reserve banks, there are twelve Federal Reserve districts and each one has a federal reserve bank. Each Federal Reserve district often comprises multiple states. Those are district banks that provide liquidity to banks within their districts. The Board of Governors also tracks economic statistics from each Federal Reserve district. Today these are the same districts as when they were created one hundred years ago with the Federal Reserve Act of 1913. Each member of the Board of Governors is nominated by the President and is confirmed by the United States Senate. The Chairman of the Federal Reserve serves as the figurehead of the Fed. The Chairman is a regular member of the Board of Governors, who serve fourteen years each. Each member of the Board of Governors gets one vote, including the Chairman.

In the Federal Reserve district banks there are nine members serving on a board for each bank. They are in three different classes of membership; there are Class A, Class B and Class C members. Class A members are chosen by regional banks shareholders. They work to represent bank interests in the Federal Reserve district. Class B members are also chosen by the shareholders of the regional banks, yet these members are supposed to represent the interests of the public, not their respective banks. The Board of Governors in Washington nominates class C board members. These people are also supposed to represent the interests of the public. There are member banks that are private banks that own stock in its Regional Federal Reserve Bank. Even national banks own shares of stock in a least one Federal Reserve district bank. Almost half of the banks in the country own shares in a Regional Federal Reserve Bank. These shares cannot be sold or traded and for a bank to own shares the share value must be equal to three percent of it's combined capital. In exchange for the ownership of shares, banks can vote for six of the nine members of the Regional Federal Reserve Board.

The Federal Reserve was created to address different problems that face the economy. It was created to address banking panics, to supervise and regulate private banks, manage the countries money supply, provide liquidity when banks needed it. The Federal Reserve was given a triple mandate by the Congress in the 1970s. They are supposed to use monetary policy to achieve price stability, achieve moderate long-term interest rates and achieve maximum employment. The Federal Reserve sets an interest rate called the overnight rate or is called the federal funds rate. This is the interest rate that banks charge each other when one institution loans money to another institution. This interest rate has a large impact on interest rates overall. The higher this interest rate, the more expensive it is for banks to borrow money from each other. This slows down lending and causes banks to raise the interest payments they give depositors. The Federal Reserve also has what is called the discount window. This allows banks and financial institutions to borrow directly from the Federal Reserve, the interest rate that the Federal Reserve charges is called the discount rate, repo rate or base rate. This rate is always higher than the federal funds rate because the Federal Reserve is called the lender of last resort, they don't want to encourage banks to borrow from the Fed. They want banks to borrow from each other before they come to the Fed for a short-term loan. Banks and financial institutions encounter liquidity problems and they will borrow from the Federal Reserve if they cannot borrow enough from other private banks and institutions. The Federal Reserve does not want to lend money to financial institutions if they don't have to, they don't want the Fed to become too financially exposed or have too many liabilities that would imperil the Fed and their mission.

When interest rates are higher, more people opt to put their money in the bank to safely get the interest. The higher the interest rate that the bank pays you to keep your money in their bank, the more likely it is that you will give them your money. This higher rate of interest is safe; you don't have to worry about losing your money like you would in the stock market or the risk of any other investment. The higher interest rates cause there to be less money in the stock market and also results in less money being spent on goods and services in the economy. The higher interest rates cause interest rates on car loans and mortgages to go up. This makes it more expensive for people to borrow money. The higher interest payments means that fewer people will borrow money and the ones who do have less money to spend on other things. Higher interest rates hurt businesses too because it causes the interest that they pay for business loans to increase. If a business has to pay more for a business loan, they are going to have lower profits. This will also result in fewer businesses getting business loans because it is too expensive. All of these factors make the economy slow down. There is less buying, less business activity, and the overall economy slows down or even goes into a recession if the interest rates are too high.

The opposite of all of these things happens when the Federal Reserve lowers the Federal funds rate. The Fed usually does this when the economy is in a recession or when economic growth or inflation threatens to be negative. The lower fed funds rate causes other interest rates from one-month

Treasury bonds up to thirty-year Treasury bond yields or interest rates to go lower too. That makes it

cheaper for people to borrow money to buy a car or a house. It also makes it cheaper for businesses to

borrow money. Lower costs of borrowing puts more money in peoples pockets to spend or save. This

helps increase economic growth and inflation. With a low interest rate, people are tempted to take their

money out of their savings account at the bank. This is because they are earning little or no interest and

may put some of their money in the stock market instead. People may decide to invest their money in

something else like real estate, commodities or even a business. Lower interest rates increase economic

growth and incentivizes people and businesses to invest and spend more money. The Federal Reserve

will lower the over-night rate or federal funds rate, which also makes it cheaper for banks to borrow

money from each other. That increases liquidity throughout the banking system and makes it a lot easier

for them to loan out money to customers. Lower interest rates helps banks lower interest rates they

charge their customers and it helps banks get the money they need easier.


Why would the Fed raise interest rates? Why would they raise interest rates so high that it would

cause a recession? Everyone knows how unpleasant those things are for everyone. There is another thing

that the Fed is trying to stop which is also unpleasant, high rates of inflation. Inflation is when the

general level of prices increases over time. This includes everything from food at the grocery store to

home values to the price of gasoline. There is a so-called basket of goods that contain average items that

people buy to calculate inflation. This inflation rate is called the CPI or the Consumer Price Index. The

CPI and the rate of inflation have become synonymous. This is used as a basis for cost of living

increases and determining the general level of prices for consumers. Historically inflation has increased

by around two-three percent per year on average over the last hundred years. That is the level that the

Federal Reserve would call ideal. It's not too low, not too high. Low stable inflation is the ideal

outcome. If inflation is above four percent, the vicious cycle of escalating inflation may begin. High inflation is damaging to the economy and to the average person. Zero or negative inflation is called deflation and this is when inflation declines over the course of a year. It may sound good in theory, but it discourages people from consuming and can put the economy in a trap that is difficult to get out of. America experienced severe deflation during the Great Depression; it was one of the reasons why it was so bad.

The reason that the Federal Reserve raises interest rates is when inflation gets too high, they are supposed to achieve price stability. Typically when the economy is growing fast the rate of inflation accelerates because a good economy has an upward impact on prices. It makes it easier for companies to raise prices and pass off their increased costs onto consumers. More people are working when the economy is doing well; this greatly increases demand for goods and services, which also allows companies to increase prices. When the economy is strong unemployment is typically low, this means that the demand for labor is high and the supply of labor is low. This results in workers being able to demand wage increases. The price of labor goes up when the supply of it is low and the demand for it is high. Increasing wages is one of the biggest factors that cause inflation. It is also very expensive for companies to do; workers are their biggest expense. Employees are usually around 60-70% of the cost of doing business. If companies have to raise wages, they will increase the prices of the goods and services they offer. They want to pass along as much of those costs as possible to their customers (They do the same thing with taxes). The reason is about maximizing profitability, which is why businesses exist in the first place. There are also inflation expectations. If people expect inflation to be high in the future they are more likely to buy things now instead of waiting. If the same thing will cost a lot more in a year, why wouldn't someone buy it now for less? If there are expectations that inflation will be higher in the future, workers will demand an increase in their wages in their contracts. If workers think inflation will be five percent over the next year, they will demand at least a five percent increase in their wages. These factors can lead to higher inflation for the overall economy. These factors feed on other factors and can create a vicious cycle of higher and higher inflation. This happened in America in the 1970s with inflation that was at 6% in 1969 rising to a post war record rate of inflation that peaked in 1980 at 13.5%. In order to prevent these kinds of situations the Federal Reserve steps in by raising interest rates.

The other mandate that Congress has created is for the Federal Reserve to provide stability for the US Dollar. They do that by ensuring that inflation is not too low or too high. They do that by ensuring that interest rates do not stay too low or too high for too long. The Federal Reserve is juggling these different sometimes-competing objectives of maximum employment, high sustainable GDP growth, low inflation, and stable interest rates. These things serve to support the underlying economy and the stability of the Dollar. The Federal Reserve works to keep these various things in balance and have the long run goal of assuring that the overall economy is as strong and well functioning as possible. The Federal Reserve has not always done a prefect job of this. There was a colossal failure by the Federal Reserve in the early 1930's which helped create the Great Depression. The Federal Reserve was committed to defending the gold standard. As a result, between 1930 and March of 1933 the Federal Reserve reduced the monetary supply by 1/3 and this resulted in prices declining by 1/3. That means the Fed created severe deflation, which was a critical factor in creating the Great Depression. Due to the severe deflation it was impossible for debtors to pay their debt back, consumers postponed all purchases to get a lower price, banks failed because debtors couldn't afford to pay back their loans and there were bank runs. That caused credit to disappear and a vicious cycle of ever collapsing economic demand and job losses caused the economy to implode until FDR declared a banking holiday and got rid of the gold standard. The second major Fed failure was in the 1970's when the country experienced a decade of record inflation partly because of the Fed's mistakes, this is mainly because the Fed had no experience in battling inflation before the 1970s. The third crisis for the Fed was the financial crisis in the fall of 2008 and disgust with how the Federal Reserve has managed things ever since.

The Federal Reserve has a lot of influence in maintaining the stability of the American currency. Before the early 1970's, the United States Dollar was fixed at a rate of 1/35$^{th}$ an ounce of gold. In the 1930's after taking the United States off of the gold standard, President Roosevelt made it illegal for the average person to own gold (it was only legal for people to use it in the arts). He set a price of $35 dollars an ounce to encourage people to turn in their gold to the federal government. Thirty-five dollars an ounce was far higher than the free market price of an ounce of gold in the 1930's. This is why Fort Knox was created in Kentucky to house the gold of the federal government in 1937. In the 1960's, $35 dollars an ounce was a lot lower than the free market price of gold. Foreign governments who deposited their gold into the United States were withdrawing their gold from the country. Private investors who kept their gold in the United States were also withdrawing their gold. The United States gold supply was dwindling by the early 1970's. President Richard Nixon sought to end this problem. He did so by getting rid of the gold standard. This made it legal for private citizens in America to own gold again and it made gold into a commodity like oil or pork bellies. This allowed gold to be traded on the open markets. The dollar was made into a commodity of sorts because it also began to be traded on the open markets in the 1970's. This is called a free-floating currency. To this day, the Dollar is a free-floating currency that trades every day throughout the world. The dynamic of supply and demand affects the value of the dollar by letting it be traded. In 1971 the fixed exchange ended with the Bretton Woods system. The Bretton Woods system was created in Bretton Woods, New Hampshire in 1944. This created the framework for free-world markets in the postwar world. This made fixed currencies the norm in the world economy. All countries that participated in the Bretton Woods system pegged their currency to the American Dollar. The Bretton Woods system set up a system of rules, laws, and procedures to govern the global monetary system. The IMF and the World Bank were created out of the Bretton Woods summit. The G.A.T.T. or the General Agreement on Tariffs and Trade was created in 1948 and the W.T.O. or the World Trade Organization replaced it in 1995.

The Federal Reserve is a very powerful institution. They have a lot of control over the economy and they possess the ability to buy trillions of dollars in assets whether they are bonds, mortgages, stocks and other assets to influence the economy. For better or worse the Federal Reserve has had this power to micromanage different aspects of the economy. For such a powerful institution, the American people have no influence over it. The Fed lacks accountability to the average American. They lack public input, transparency and operate with a veil of secrecy around their activities. At the moment members of the Federal Reserve have so much power that they rarely have to consult the American people. The Chairman of the Federal Reserve only started reporting to Congress twice a year recently. Traditionally the Chairman reported to Congress once a year and then went back to the Federal Reserve. The Federal Reserve was created in 1913; it was created long after the Constitution and the Bill of Rights were. The Supreme Court has ruled before that the Federal Reserve is constitutional, but the Founders never envisioned a Central Bank like the Fed. In light of the financial crisis we need to re-examine the role of the Fed and the Constitutionality of having a central bank. It's not in the Constitution either how that bank is controlled by the people. For some of the Founders the idea of a federal central bank having so much control over the country would have horrified them.

The people deserve the ability to elect members of the Federal Reserve. The people don't have any power over the Federal Reserve today. Members of the Board of Governors in Washington should be on a national ballot and be subjected to elections by the American people. They currently have terms of fourteen years. Each member of the Board of Governors should be subjected to four-year terms instead, they should have term limits and only be permitted to serve for two four-year terms. This is what would apply to members of the Senate, the President, and members of the Federal Courts. In the twelve regional Federal Reserve banks, members of those nine person committees should also be subjected to elections and term limits. They would have four-year terms with a two-term limit. The people that live in each Federal Reserve district should be able to vote for members of the nine person committees for their regions Federal Reserve Bank. The Federal Reserve districts need to be changed to reflect the major changes over the last hundred years. Members of these nine person boards would be subjected to regional elections as opposed to national elections for members of the Board of Governors in Washington DC. Currently, banks and the President have far too much power in deciding who gets to serve in the Federal Reserve. The American people have no power over who gets to serve. The process is closed off to many people that could serve yet are not even considered by the powers at be.

If the people could elect members of the Federal Reserve it would open up the process to many people that currently would never be considered. There are plenty of qualified people who would perform honorably and serve well but who never have the opportunity in the current system. If there were elections anyone could run to serve on the Federal Reserve, either for a Regional bank or the Board of Governors in Washington. This would greatly open up the process and give the people a choice in who actually serves. The public would benefit by having a variety of people to choose from. There is a constantly revolving door between Wall Street and Washington DC, people go from being on Wall Street to serving in a government job in Washington or people begin serving in Washington and then go on to get a high paying job on Wall Street. This creates a conflict of interest between the Federal Reserve and regulators on one side and Wall Street and the private sector on the other side. The regulators are often people that worked on Wall Street and have plenty of friends there. This causes the Federal Reserve and regulatory agencies to be heavily influenced by the banks and financial institutions that they regulate. Elections would be a way of addressing this problem. While there is the constant interplay between the regulators in Washington and Wall Street the average person is ignored in this current circumstance. For such a powerful institution as the Federal Reserve the American people have no oversight over it at all. There is a lot of corruption and issues with conflicts of interest. The regulators are either people who used to be employed by those they are regulating or the regulators are people who hope to work for the people they are regulating in the future. Banks and other private interests heavily influence the members of the Federal Reserve. They are also heavily influenced by the politicians that serve in Washington. In between Wall Street, financial institutions and politicians in Congress the American people don't stand any chance at having any influence under the status quo. Americans get to elect people to Congress and get to elect the President, but those politicians receive millions of dollars in campaign contributions from banks, financial institutions and Wall Street. Because of that the President and the Senators would never let anyone on the Federal Reserve that those campaign contributors did not approve of. This causes corporations and special interests to have a lot of control over the Federal Reserve (Not to mention the Federal Government in general). The people deserve to elect members of the various Federal Reserve boards. These people should be working for the people instead of these private interests, special interests, and politicians in Washington.

The banks should not select the people who serve on the Federal Reserve boards. Banks should not own shares in the Federal Reserve banks either. Banks have too much power in the country as it is with the Congress, the President and state politicians. They should not have so much influence over the Federal Reserve that they are the ones who select its board members. It's especially outrageous when three of the members of the board for each Regional Federal Reserve bank are chosen by the banks, yet those particular board members are supposed to look out for the interests of the public. The banks and financial institutions have their own private agendas. Sometimes their private interests go against the interests of the public and what would make sound economic policy. Banks should have some kind of a relationship with the Federal Reserve to ensure that the banking system is sound and that the Fed can do their job. Yet the banks have too much power when they can choose people that make policy at the Fed. Some of the people that serve in these regional Federal Reserve banks go on to work in the private sector after. If they do a "good job" working for a banks particular interest then they may get hired there after. This represents a further conflict of interest. Members of the Regional Federal Reserve boards sometimes go on to serve on the Federal Reserve Board in Washington. First of all, they have to be nominated by the President. The President receives millions of dollars in campaign contributions from banks and financial institutions. The President is not going to offend those people by nominating someone that is critical of them or who will work against their interests. Even if the President did, Senators would not vote for someone like that. This is because most of them receive millions of dollars in campaign contributions from banks and financial institutions. From deciding the kind of people who can get nominated to serve on the Board of Governors, to the fact that banks get to select members of the regional Federal Reserve boards, to the issue that most who serve in the Federal Reserve either came from a bank or want to work at one after they leave, the banks have a lot of power over the Federal Reserve system. Since they have a tremendous amount of power over the Fed, they would invariably lose power if the Federal Reserve board members were elected. That power would go to the American people who have the most at stake when it comes to inflation, the dollar and the economy in general. The people that have the most at stake deserve more involvement with the Fed and they deserve more information about what the Fed does and what their policies are. The Fed should be forced to explain and defend their policies to the public so that the people are better informed about what is going on with the economy. The Federal Reserve would be a more popular institution if the American people understood it better.

If members of the Federal Reserve boards were elected it would open up the process. It would bring much needed transparency to a part of the federal government that possesses a large amount of power. It's not merely political power as much as it is power over the American economy. That affects the lives of the American people in very personal and real ways. Yet the people have no control over this extremely powerful part of the government and the people lack any check over this part of the government either. Our system is supposed to be about checks and balances between the different branches of the federal government. The Federal Reserve is a relatively new idea that was only created one hundred years ago. There is a large degree of secrecy around the Federal Reserve System. It is closed off to the American people and it involves a complex process of running the economy. Not only does the average person have no control over the Federal Reserve, they also don't understand it too well and lack information about it. The way that the Federal Reserve runs is counter to the idea of transparency. Electing members of the regional Federal Reserve boards and the Federal Reserve Board in Washington would bring about an increased level of transparency that would inform the American people about their activities and intentions.

The average person is not terribly happy with the Federal Reserve these days. There have been calls to get rid of the Federal Reserve completely and there are people who support the idea of having no central bank of any kind. There are others that favor keeping the Federal Reserve the way that is but bring about some cosmetic reforms. Instead of getting rid of it entirely, the people should be allowed to decide who is on the Federal Reserve boards. Giving the people control over who gets to serve would allow them to have a Fed that was responsive to their needs and concerns. It would give the people much more information about the Federal Reserve and Fed policy. It would give the people a Federal Reserve that was doing what was in the best interest of the economy and their lives instead of an institution that has been captured by Wall Street. Another benefit of electing members of the Federal Reserve would be that it would open up the process to many candidates that currently have no chance of getting on. Anybody could get elected to serve on a regional or the Federal Reserve board in Washington. There are many qualified people who could serve well that are never given the opportunity. They either don't share the political ideology of the President or the Senate. Or they have some unorthodox positions that cause special interests in Washington to destroy their chances of getting nominated. Any person that would in any way threaten the established interests in Washington or Wall Street would never have any chance of getting nominated. Some of these people are the people who are the best for the job and would serve the economy and the people the best, yet they are not allowed to serve because there are too many roadblocks in Washington. The Federal Reserve would benefit by having fresh blood and new people that could serve. The agency would have plenty of qualified people who would serve honorably and serve the interests of the Federal Reserve well. There are many qualified people that have no chance of getting nominated for a variety of reasons. If the people could elect Federal Reserve board members it would allow anyone to run. The relatively closed process would be open to many different candidates that for whatever reason would be unable to nominated by the President or confirmed by the Senate. The people would benefit by having a choice as to what kind of person they would like to serve. They could choose somebody that better understood their lives and their economic realities. Elections would make the Federal Reserve accountable to the American people. This is instead of the status quo where they are more accountable to politicians in Congress, special interests and Wall Street.

The Federal Reserve should be more accountable to the people. We are the ones who live in the real world and have to bear the consequences of Fed policy. Some may wonder whether the people are capable of choosing members of the Regional and Federal Reserve Boards. Some may wonder whether politicizing the process may harm the interests of the people and the economy. Some may wonder if the current system would be better than a new system where members of the various Federal Reserve Boards were elected. Some may wonder if we even need a Federal Reserve System at all while we are at attempting to reform the system so much. These are all legitimate questions. There are plenty of other legitimate questions as well. The Federal Reserve System is a complicated and controversial system these days. Since they possess so much power, are under so much influence from banks, and are so little understood by the people, the Federal Reserve System needs to be subjected to more transparency and control from the American people. The people should be able to elect whom they please to serve on the Regional and the Federal Reserve Board in Washington. Banks should not have a virtual monopoly over deciding who serves. Members of the Federal Reserve Boards should also be subjected to term limits. This would be two four-year terms at the maximum that each person could serve. Since each person would be subjected to term limits they would not have to face re-election to the Fed again in their second term, this would preserve some independence for the Federal Reserve. This is the same as it is for members of the Senate, the President, and would be for members of the federal courts. Members of the House of Representatives have two-year terms, but they could also be there for only eight years.

There are some other potential problems with electing members of the Federal Reserve and having term limits in place. One of them would be the economy may suffer in the long run by having such a political central bank. The people would vote in people that pursued populist policies that harmed the economy. That's a potential concern with electing members of the Federal Reserve. But the American people would be able to decide who served on the various Federal Reserve boards. The American people want low unemployment, strong economic growth, a strong dollar, stable prices and a well functioning US economy. They would vote in people that would pursue those policies where the economy would do better in the long run than it has in the past. The people are eminently capable of selecting people to serve on the various Federal Reserve boards. They live in the real world and would demand a Federal Reserve that pursued their interests. If the economy were not performing well the people would be able to get rid of Federal Reserve members that they did not support and support new people that would change Fed policy. That would cause the Fed to chart a course correction in the event that they were failing to keep the economy to the peoples satisfaction. The current situation allows the banks, politicians and special interests to have more influence and control over the Federal Reserve. There are times that they pursue their own narrow private interests over the interests of the US economy. The Federal Reserve should be about serving the American people and doing what is best for the US economy.

Another potential problem is that with term limits, there may not be enough experienced people running the Federal Reserve. Without adequate experience, wouldn't the American people be poorly served? Some may worry that term limits would make it so the Fed was poorly run and that the US economy would suffer. With term limits in place a member of the Federal Reserve could serve for two

four-year terms. They would be able to serve on the board of a Federal Reserve district for two terms

and then the Federal Reserve board in Washington for two terms. That would total sixteen years that

somebody would be able to serve on a Federal Reserve board. Currently, members are elected to

fourteen-year terms so they would be able to serve longer than they do now, but they would have to win

four elections in order to do that instead of zero. Term limits would allow people with adequate

experience to run for a position on a Federal Reserve board. The American people would be able to

select candidates that they found to be most qualified for the job. There would be no shortage of

qualified people that wanted to serve in the Federal Reserve. For the most part the voters would elect

people that understood economics much less monetary policy so they could execute responsible Fed

policy. The best candidates would be the people that could explain the Fed and what their policies were

to the average voter. If they can make the average person understand than that is proof that they know it

well themselves. A lot of people try to make everything seem so complicated that you can't understand

what they are talking about. The people that truly understand something can explain it to anybody. The

voters deserve more information about the Fed and more people that can articulate Fed policy. The Fed

is not well understood by the public and that causes a lot of misinformation to spread and creates major

misconceptions about the Fed. The people deserve a Fed that explains itself and defends its policies,

especially because they are supposed to do what is in our interests and the economys interest. Having a

mysterious institution feeds into peoples worst fears about the Fed and their real intentions.


The next possible problem with subjecting the Fed to elections is that the Fed gets extremely

political and conducts policy that hurts the economy. They might always cut interest rates before every

election in order to please voters. That could cause inflation to spiral out of control like what happened

in the 1970s. The Fed could be trapped in a cycle where they raise rates to bring down inflation and then

when the next election is coming they cut interest rates to please the voters and get re-elected. After the election they raise rates again and go back and forth for every election, this process would reduce Fed credibility, which would cause inflation expectations to increase. That could cause an endless cycle of high and escalating inflation. Fed policy may change wildly along with shifts in the ever-changing political winds. This is a nightmare scenario that would not come to pass. First of all the Federal Reserve Boards would have staggered terms which would preserve Fed independence and prevent all members from being subjected to elections at the same time. This would allow the Fed to conduct monetary policy and not produce wild or unpredictable outcomes. Secondly, people serving on the Federal Reserve Board would be determined to conduct sound monetary policy. They would pursue their multiple mandates of a stable dollar, low stable inflation, full employment and strong sustainable economic growth. In the 1970s the Fed had no experience of fighting inflation so it escalated throughout the period, today people at the Fed know how to prevent inflation from getting out of control and how to fight inflation that is too high. The American people would not want inflation to be too high and would support Fed policy that produced the best overall economy. The majority of the people would reward a Board member for a well performing economy and this would act as a further incentive to conduct proper monetary policy. Even if there were politicians elected to the Federal Reserve board they would still have to vote in a committee. If someone too radical or political got elected the rest of the committee would outvote them. There will be other Board members that will be able to prevent radical and unpredictable outcomes from the Fed. Elections would require the Fed to explain the reasoning behind their policies to the public and raise support for them. The Federal Reserve is bound to attract people that want to serve the public and aren't as concerned about a political career. It would attract people that were not as concerned about staying in power for years and instead would want to conduct legitimate monetary policy. They would want to serve the country well and be more willing to conduct the right policy even if they lose their reelection. The Federal Reserve would fail to attract so many career politicians because it is not a very powerful position and if anything serving on the Federal Reserve Board is more likely to end a political career rather than advance one. This is not a very popular institution and it is a lot more at the mercy of how the economy does than most people think. More people that served on the Federal Reserve Board may only want to be there for one term anyway. They would want a way of giving back to the country and bringing their expertise to benefit the Fed and the economy in general. Term limits would also help preserve Fed independence so they could be free to conduct monetary policy that was best for the economy and overall society.

If the Fed is subjected to elections than members of the Federal Reserve board are turned into politicians. Wouldn't they become like Congressman and other politicians who desperately want political power? Wouldn't they compromise Fed policy in order for them to get reelected? This is a real possibility but there are several reasons why that is unlikely to happen. One is that there is not too much power available to someone serving on the Federal Reserve. The lack of power or great perks with that job will make it a less desirable job for ambitious people. The second reason why Fed board members will not turn into politicians is that running the Fed is a politically dangerous job. Since it is all about managing the economy whenever a recession happens or something else goes wrong everyone will blame the Federal Reserve. The voters will take it out on the Board members up for reelection. That would make the job undesirable and serving on the Federal Reserve Board would be more likely to destroy your political career rather than advance it. The third thing is that term limits and intense public scrutiny would make this a difficult job to have where someone wouldn't have very much power. Considering the above reasons it is highly likely that people getting elected to the Federal Reserve boards would be doing it at the end of their careers. They would have knowledge and years of experience and they would want to give something back to the country. Since the job would be more likely to attract and the voters would be more likely to pick people like this is another factor which will maintain Fed independence. These reasons along with the fact that the voters would select competent people for the job are why the Fed would not be populated with politicians like Congress. Even if politicians got elected to serve on the Federal Reserve Board or a regional board they would be subjected to term limits. People like that would not be permitted to serve for more than eight years and they would leave and move on to some other political office that they could run for. Just because a politician may get elected to a Federal Reserve Board does not automatically mean that they will do a poor job. They might be under more pressure to do a responsible job than other members because they are desperate to move up the political ladder and get a more lucrative and powerful job.

Another issue with electing members of the Federal Reserve is that special interests could capture them. Since people running to serve on a Federal Reserve Board would need money to run their campaigns, they would be forced to raise money from special interests, Wall Street, corporations, etc. This is a real possibility but candidates would be under heavy public scrutiny when they were subjected to elections. The people would get to make the ultimate decision as to who would be permitted to serve and who couldn't. In reality the candidates would need to raise money in order to run a campaign and win a campaign, they would end up having to raise money from banks, hedge funds and Wall Street. Banks and Wall Street would not support all of the candidates, there would be plenty of candidates running that either didn't meet their standards or who would openly oppose them and would run against them. It's questionable whether a Wall Street backed candidate would be able to win in an election these days. Most people hate Wall Street and the Federal Reserve and would be looking to elect new people that would come in and change things. If the public knew that a candidate received heavy Wall Street backing that very well might discredit those candidates. The public would be aware of who gave money to the candidates and they would be against people that received large campaign contributions from Wall Street or financial institutions. Banks would donate millions of dollars to various candidates so that they could maintain control over the Federal Reserve (Just like how they control Congress and the Presidency). Being a Wall Street backed candidate would be a scarlet letter that would make it difficult to get elected. Elections would open up the possibility of putting people on the Federal Reserve boards that would not be captured by Wall Street and banks. Not every person elected will be free of influence or control from those financiers, but this alternative would be far superior to the current situation where nearly every member of the Federal Reserve Boards are captured. Since the President selects every person that is up for consideration on the Federal Reserve Board in Washington, they will never pick anybody that would upset their large Wall Street supporters. Even if they did they would still have to have their nominee confirmed by the US Senate. A majority of Senators would never support any nominee that their Wall Street supporters didn't like either. With elections the people would be able to pick somebody who was not in Wall Streets pocket or who hoped to be in the future. Wall Street backed candidates would be allowed to run but its unlikely that many voters would support those candidates.

If members of the Federal Reserve Boards are subjected to elections wouldn't Wall Street, Banks and financial institutions still control the Federal Reserve? They would donate as much money as they could to their chosen candidates who would have a good chance of getting elected with their large campaign war chests. Their candidates would win and keep running the Fed. Wouldn't this keep things the same as they are now? This is a very real possibility that Wall Street will be able to deploy enough cash to buy the elections for their chosen candidates. There could be strict campaign finance rules or limits that would prevent them from being able to continue to control the Fed. There could be other ways that their influence could be reduced to assure an open and fair electoral process. Even without campaign finance rules or other limits the public would not support candidates that came away with heavy campaign contributions from Wall Street. Wall Street is so reviled today that it would be an asset for any candidate to declare that they received no campaign contributions from banks and Wall Street. It would benefit candidates who didn't receive money from them and it would harm candidates who received contributions. Elections would ultimately put the people in charge and let them decide who they want serving on the various Federal Reserve Boards. If they found a candidate that had a heavy Wall Street background and received millions of dollars to run their campaign from Wall Street and they liked them they would be free to elect them. Elections would be about putting the American people in charge, it would be their power to elect whoever they felt was most qualified for the job. Elections would not remove all influence that Wall Street and banks have on the Fed but it would give the public much more control over the Fed than they have now. The current situation is where the banks and Wall Street have near total control whereas elections would give the public a huge increase in control over the Federal Reserve.

With elections for the members of the Federal Reserve Boards wouldn't there still be a conflict of interest? Candidates would more than likely be people that worked on Wall Street or for a major bank at one time or they may want to work on Wall Street in the future. This would mean that these people would be afraid of offending banks, Wall Street firms and other financial institutions so they would serve in a way that benefitted those institutions. People that used to work on Wall Street would have connections with Wall Street and would hesitate to regulate them too stringently or do anything else to go against them. This is a conflict of interest problem that already exists with the Federal Reserve, the Securities and Exchange Committee (SEC) and other regulatory agencies. Along with the fact that Wall Street donates to the President and Senators campaigns, this gives the banks and financial institutions control over the Federal Reserve. If the board members were subjected to elections it would give the people control over deciding who can serve on the Fed and that would greatly reduce the power that Wall Street had over the Federal Reserve. Elections would allow the voters to pick people that did not have a career on Wall Street or for a financial institution. They could also pick people that were later in their careers who did not want to work on Wall Street in the future. Elections would reduce the conflict of interest problem that currently plagues the Federal Reserve Board and the other regulatory agencies. Elections wouldn't solve all of the problems that currently exist but they would mitigate them.

Some people may worry that the Federal Reserve would not conduct proper monetary policy if they were elected. This is a reason given as to why the Federal Reserve should have political independence. If members of the Federal Reserve were elected, they would still be required to do their job. Elections would also be staggered. If the people were unhappy with what the Federal Reserve was doing, the members would not all be up for re-election in the same year. This would help preserve Fed independence. If members of the Federal Reserve did a poor job then they would not get re-elected. They would also lose out on future political opportunities. The Federal Reserve would be under additional pressure to do things that benefited the economy and the average person by being subjected to elections. The members of the Federal Reserve Boards would be under more pressure to get out ahead of potential problems like deflation, recession or hyperinflation. Under the status quo, members of the Federal Reserve may possess too much independence from the people and are not aggressive enough in preventing negative outcomes for the economy and the people. Elections would force members of the Federal Reserve to defend their policies to the people. If their policies are so good for the economy, then they should be able to strongly defend those policies in front of the American people.

The American people are perfectly capable of choosing who gets to serve in the Federal Reserve. Some may worry that the American people are not qualified to choose who would best serve. If the people are deemed competent enough to elect the people who choose most who serve on the Federal Reserve boards, then they are certainly competent enough to decide who should serve themselves. It should be a decision that is taken out of politician's hands and given to the people. The average person is the one who has to live with the consequences of Fed policy. The average person is affected by high inflation, a recession, and high interest rates. They should be allowed to have a say in who serves and what direction Fed policy should go in. The Federal Reserve would not be too politicized by allowing people to elect members. The people would benefit by being able to exercise control over the Federal Reserve System and give the Fed the incentive to do what is good for the economy. The economy may sound abstract to the average person. Yet the economy is made up of all of us collectively, sound

Fed policy that benefits the economy benefits the American people. Instead of the status quo where the

Federal Reserve is secretive and many people do not understand it or its function, we should increase

transparency. The American people would benefit by learning more about the Federal Reserve System

and the members would be beholden to the people instead of banks and politicians. Since each member

would be elected to two four-year terms, they would have to get re-elected and would be under

considerable pressure to serve in the interests of the people. Those who feel that the American people

are not qualified to decide who serves on the Federal Reserve must admit that they are better trusted

with the task than those that are pursuing their own private or political interests. Part of making America

into a democracy is assuring that the American people actually control their own government, the

Federal Reserve is a large part of that government.


The Federal Reserve has a lot of power. They control the money supply, interest rates, regulate

banks, influence the dollar and the economy in general. This part of the federal government has a

tremendous amount of power while the average person has no control over it at all. Only the President

and the members of the Senate can decide who gets to serve on the Federal Reserve boards. Banks that

are members of a regional Federal Reserve Bank get to choose some members of those Federal Reserve

Boards. Banks and politicians in Washington dominate the process of selecting those who get to serve in

the Federal Reserve. This is power that should be given to the average person instead. Electing members

would provide unprecedented transparency to the Federal Reserve and the process of selecting members.

It would also allow any person to run to serve on the Federal Reserve. Currently the process is closed off

to those that could challenge the interests of politicians, special interests and the banks. Electing

members of the Federal Reserve would be an excellent opportunity to educate people about what exactly

the Fed does. Members of the Federal Reserve boards should be subjected to term limits as well; they

should not be permitted to serve indefinitely. This would go a long way toward giving the American

146

people control over their own government. This would be an indispensible aspect of making America into a democracy. In the next chapter I will discuss why we should get rid of the Electoral College and why political parties should have their primary for President on the same day in a national primary.

# Chapter Seven

The next step in the process of turning America into a democracy would be to get rid of the Electoral College. It may seem like a benign institution that allows a Presidential candidate to win the election if they win 270 Electoral College votes. The Electoral College results have gone in tandem with the popular vote in every election for President except three. Yet that is the rule in Presidential elections, a presidential candidate only has to win 270 Electoral College votes in order to win the election, they don't have to win the popular vote in order to win the election and become president. The American people should get to decide who wins the election for President. Whoever receives the largest number of votes for President should win. The Electoral College should not reign supreme over the will of the American voters. It's not very democratic that the Electoral College can do that; this part of the system needs to change. The Electoral College was a development that allowed the country to be formed in the 1787 Constitutional Convention, but it is not something that is needed any longer. The US Constitution did not and still does not require any popular vote be conducted for President at all. Getting rid of the Electoral College would be a crucial step in instituting a popular vote for President in the Constitution that would allow the people to determine the winner. This chapter is also about why the political parties should hold national primaries. All of the states primaries to nominate someone for President should take place on the same day.

During the Constitutional Convention in 1787 there was a plan put forward by Virginia that would have the Congress elect the President and Vice President. Most delegates supported this idea, but there was a committee of eleven that was formed to make recommendations for how to elect the President and Vice President. This committee recommended that instead of Congress deciding, there should be another group of people apportioned by the states in the same way that their representatives in Congress are. Each states legislature would decide who their states electors were. Some of the founders were concerned that the Congress would be too powerful if they selected the President, so they wanted to create an alternative body selected by state legislatures that would mirror their states representation in Congress. Some of the Founders wanted the President to be popularly elected; yet it was not to be because of slavery. These two parts of the Constitution explain the Electoral College.

Article II, Section 1, Clause 2 of the Constitution states:

"Each State shall appoint, in such Manner as the Legislature thereof may direct, a Number of Electors, equal to the whole Number of Senators and Representatives to which the State may be entitled in the Congress: but no Senator or Representative, or Person holding an Office of Trust or Profit under the United States, shall be appointed an Elector."

Article II, Section 1, Clause 4 of the Constitution states:

"The Congress may determine the Time of choosing the Electors, and the Day on which they shall give their Votes; which Day shall be the same throughout the United States."

In the beginning the Electoral College was created to determine the President and Vice President. The person who won the most votes became President; the person who received the second highest number of votes became Vice President. The President and Vice President were not elected by the voters but by electors who were given to each state based off of their number of representatives in Congress. Today there are 538 electors which is equal to 435 members of the House plus 100 Senators plus three electors representing Washington DC. According to the Constitution, members of the Electoral College were authorized to vote for two names for President. The two-vote ballot was made to create the greatest possibility that someone would receive votes from a majority of the electors nationwide. The founders anticipated that each state would use the district system of allocating electors and that each individual elector would exercise independent judgment when voting. The founders also expected that candidates could not pair together on the same ticket to become President and Vice President and their original intention of the Electoral College was that by design the system would rarely produce a winner and would require sending the election to Congress. The Electoral College was created to prevent the American people from being able to decide who the President was, it was intended as an anti-democratic idea from the beginning.

Under the Constitution each state government is free to decide how they choose their state electors. The Constitution only requires that those serving are not any person that is elected or appointed to federal office from being an elector. There are several different methods that the states use in order to decide. The candidates for elector are nominated by their state political parties before Election Day. In some states the electors are nominated in primaries as other candidates are nominated. In other states electors are nominated in party conventions. In some states the campaign committee of each candidate name their candidates for elector. In a presidential election 48 states and the District of Columbia employ the winner takes all method of awarding electors in a bloc. Maine and Nebraska have made recent changes to how they select their states electors; they employ the congressional district method, which selects an elector within each congressional district by popular vote. The remaining two electors are awarded based off of the statewide popular vote. The current method of choosing electors is called the short ballot and voters choose from a list of candidates. There are not many states that actually list on the ballot the names of the proposed electors. In some states if somebody wants to write someone in for President they have to write in the names of proposed electors too.

Federal elections are held on the first Tuesday after the first Monday of the month of November, it's not the first Tuesday even though the first day of the month can be a Tuesday. State political parties choose their electors in the months leading up to Election Day. After each election is over each state prepares seven certificates of Ascertainment. Each certificate represents the list of candidates for President and Vice President, their pledged electors along with the total number of votes that each candidate received. The certificates of ascertainment are mandated to carry their states official seal and the signature of the Governor, these documents are sent to the National Archivist in Washington DC as soon as possible after the election is over.

The Electoral College was not called the Electoral College by the Founders. The Constitution refers to them as Electors and the phrase Electoral College was not written into federal law until 1845. The electors don't actually meet in person as a group, the electors meet in their state capitals on the Monday after the second Wednesday in December. That is when they cast their electoral votes on separate ballots for President and Vice President. All states have a slightly different way of doing it but all states engage in a similar series of steps and the Congress has the constitutional authority to regulate the procedures the states follow. Each meeting of electors is opened by the election certification official, usually it is the states secretary of state who reads the Certificate of Ascertainment. The Certificate of Ascertainment is the document that describes who was chosen to cast the electoral votes. Each elector that is present answers to his or her name and any vacancies are noted in writing. The next step is when a president or chairman of the meeting is selected, occasionally there is a vice chairman. The electors often choose a secretary who takes notes during the meeting. In most states at this part of the meeting political officials give speeches. After the speeches the time for balloting has arrived, this is when the electors choose one or two people to act as tellers. Tellers are assigned to count the electors votes. Some states provide for the placing in nomination of a candidate to receive the electoral votes. Each elector submits a written ballot with the name of the candidate for President. The tellers count the ballots and announce the results. The next step is casting votes for Vice President, which follows the same pattern as it does for President. Each states electors must complete six Certificates of Vote. Each Certificate of Vote must be signed by all of the electors and a Certificate of Ascertainment must be attached to each of the Certificates of Vote. Each Certificate of Vote must include the names of those who received an electoral vote for either the office of President or of Vice President. The electors certify the Certificates of Vote and copies of the Certificates are then sent in the following fashion. One is sent by registered mail to the President of the Senate (Vice President), two are sent by registered mail to the Archivist of the United States, two are sent to the states secretary of state and one is sent to the chief judge of the United States district court where those electors met. A staff member of the President of the Senate collects the Certificates of Vote as they arrive and prepares them for the joint session of the Congress. The certificates are arranged- unopened- in alphabetical order and placed in two special mahogany boxes. Alabama through Missouri is in one box and Montana through Wyoming is in the second box (The District of Columbia is in the first box).

The Electoral College is a much more complicated process than most people realize. There are even so called faithless electors. This is a person who is an elector that votes for someone other than the person pledged or does not vote for any person. Even though a faithless elector has not decided an election for President so far, twenty-four states have laws that punish faithless electors. The entire Electoral College emanates from the idea that the founders did not want the American people to select their President. They were hoping that the Electoral College would create a situation where the Congress got to decide. Polls consistently show that the American people want the right to elect their President. America would become a genuine democracy if the American people were the ultimate deciders of who became the President, one-person one vote.

The United States should get rid of the Electoral College. The Electoral College was created to create a balance between the influence of large states and small states. The result these days is that elections are narrowly decided in a handful of swing states. States with large populations like California, New York and Texas are ignored while small states like New Hampshire, Iowa, and Nevada are highly prized. The Electoral College takes the power of deciding who gets to be President away from the voters. It also causes Presidential campaigns to be focused on winning the votes of a small group of independent voters in the swing states. This process gives a disproportionate amount of influence to the swing states. The interests of most states that are not swing states are not as influential or represented as well. The American people alone should be able to decide who gets to be the President. Whoever wins the popular vote or most votes wins and then that is all. It would create a truly national campaign for the office where candidates would have an incentive to visit all fifty states during the campaign. It would even incentivize them to campaign to those that can vote in territories and other parts of the world.

The American people were not allowed to vote for President originally. The Electoral College was created to decide who the President would be. It was not until 1824 that the Popular vote for President was counted. Each state has two Senators and at least one member in the House of Representatives. This was created as a compromise during the Constitutional Convention in 1787. People who lived in colonies with small populations like Georgia, South Carolina, or Rhode Island were afraid that colonies with much larger populations like Virginia and Pennsylvania would dominate the new country. Larger colonies like New York and Virginia demanded greater influence given their larger populations. So the compromise was that there would be a House of Representatives and a Senate. The House of Representatives was based on population. Even though every state regardless of population received one member of the House, they received additional members of the House if they had a larger population. The more people that live in a state, the more representatives they have in Congress. The Senate was created to make all of the states equal, so each state received two Senators regardless of

152

how large or small their states population was. This is related to the Electoral College because this directly influences how many Electoral College votes each state has. Every state has a minimum of three Electoral College votes. This is represented by the fact that each state has two senators and one member of the House of Representatives. If a state has two senators and fifteen members in the House, then that state will have seventeen Electoral College votes. Whatever Presidential candidate wins the popular vote in a state wins the Electoral College votes of that state in a winner take all fashion. There are two states that award the electoral votes differently. Nebraska and Maine give out the Electoral College votes based off of Congressional districts instead of the entire state while the remaining two votes are awarded by the state wide popular vote. Whoever wins the popular vote in the Congressional district wins that one Electoral College vote. The Electoral College was created to give power to the states. It was also created out of a compromise that attempted to balance the power and influence that each state has in the Federal Government. Not only does that affect the design of Congress it has also affected the way we vote for President.

The Republican and Democratic parties hold a series of primaries to determine who becomes the Presidential nominee of their party. Currently, Iowa is the first state that has its caucus election for each party. Technically the first state that holds its primary is New Hampshire even though it is always after Iowa, the third is South Carolina, the fourth these days is Nevada and the fifth is Florida, Texas and Michigan on the same day. The voters in these early primary states have the power to determine what kind of candidate becomes the nominee for President. The voters in these states have way too much power in determining this outcome. If there were a national primary, all of the people who are in the Republican Party or the Democratic Party and other parties would be able to determine whom their party's nominee for President was. Those that show up to vote in the Iowa caucuses wield too much power in determining who gets to be the nominee for each party. The people of Iowa and New Hampshire have way too much influence in the process of who can become the President.

Historically the candidates that are in first in these states win their parties nomination almost every time. It actually means something to win in Iowa and then New Hampshire. Once a candidate wins those states they are impossible to stop and all of the other candidates leave the race well before a vast majority of the states have held their primary. So the effect is that the people of Iowa and New Hampshire alone get to decide who can be President in a lot of cases. There is absolutely nothing wrong with the people in Iowa, New Hampshire, South Carolina and in other early primary states. They are completely competent people that deserve a voice just as much as anyone else in America does. Yet isn't it unfair that they have so much more power than most other Americans? This proposal is simply calling for equality amongst all Americans and not giving too much power to a select few. In order to make America into a democracy, this aspect of how Presidents are chosen must change.

What usually happens in presidential primaries is that Iowa and New Hampshire are the states that are the kingmakers in most contests. Candidates who either lose these primaries or place poorly drop out of the race. This disqualifies many kinds of candidates from being able to become President. Since it is a two party system and has been throughout our history, there are only certain kinds of candidates that can become President. If you do not appeal to Iowa or New Hampshire voters then you can never become President. There are some candidates that are too socially liberal to win in Iowa; there are other candidates that are not fiscally conservative enough to win in New Hampshire. To hold national primaries would not only be fair to all Americans, it would open up the process so many candidates that could never become President under the status quo could have a reasonable chance. The voters in all of the states would have to be courted by those running for President. What voters wouldn't want the attention that Iowa and New Hampshire voters get? Yet it is unfair that only those voters receive that kind of attention. Typically after the first several primaries the other candidates have dropped out of the race and one of them is the winner. Even though that candidate has not won nearly enough delegates yet to be the nominee, it's because the other candidates realize that they have no chance of beating the front-runner and they lose donors and supporters so they drop out. The other candidates run out of money and their staffers leave their campaigns just as the party quickly unites behind the frontrunner. This makes the primaries in a vast majority of the states meaningless. It is merely a coronation for the parties soon to be nominee. This is a process that rewards a disproportionate amount of power to the voters in the early primary states. It comes at the expense of Americans in a vast majority of the country that deserve a real vote for who gets to be their parties nominee. The early states filter out many candidates who never get an opportunity to court voters in California or Massachusetts or Georgia or anywhere else. The American people deserve better than some filtered out vote that only allows them to vote for the person that voters in Iowa and New Hampshire have decided are acceptable nominees for their party.

Having a national primary for each political party is related to the Electoral College. One of the main issues with the Electoral College is that a handful of states get to determine who the next President is. The same thing is happening with primaries in each political party. Iowa, New Hampshire, South Carolina, and other early states determine the nominees of each party. That greatly reduces the list of presidential candidates down to a couple or down to the nominee. All of the people should have a fair chance at being able to decide who their party's nominee is. Some states like Iowa, New Hampshire and Florida are not only among the first states that vote in the primaries for presidential candidates, they are also swing states in the general election. They receive too much power in deciding whom each party nominates and which of those nominees actually becomes President. This creates too much focus and attention to these states. They have the ear of the President and the people who hope to become President more than the people of a vast majority of the states. This is an unfair system, it would be a more democratic process and a better course would be to allow a one day national primary and to have no Electoral College.

Most of the time the Electoral College does not have any affect on who becomes the President of the United States. In a vast majority of the elections for President, the winning candidate won the popular vote along with the Electoral College. Yet there have been three times in American history so far when the person who won the Electoral College and lost the popular vote became the President. The first time was in 1876 when Republican Civil War General Rutherford B. Hayes won the Presidency. His opponent, Democrat governor of New York Samuel Tilden won the popular vote. Since President Hayes was the first person to win the Electoral College and lose the popular vote to become the President he was referred to as his fraudulency. It is believed that a deal in Congress was reached to resolve the dispute that helped end reconstruction in exchange for Hayes being President. The second time that a candidate for President won the Electoral College and lost the popular vote was in 1888. Democrat President Grover Cleveland was running for re-election. While his Republican opponent was a former US Senator from Indiana, Benjamin Harrison. Even though Harrison lost the popular vote for President, he won the Electoral College 233-168. The third and final time so far that a candidate for President won the Electoral College and lost the popular vote was in the infamous 2000 election. Democratic candidate, Vice President Al Gore won the popular vote. While the Republican candidate, Texas governor George W. Bush won the Electoral College. The election was particularly nasty because there were a series of recounts in the pivotal state of Florida. Whoever won the state of Florida would become the President. After over a month of recounts the Supreme Court decided that the recounts must stop and George W. Bush was certified as the winner in the state of Florida along with the Presidency. He only won the state of Florida by some several hundred votes.

The first two times that a candidate for President won the Electoral College without winning the popular vote most Americans don't remember. Yet the third time in the year 2000 was certainly a bitter experience. Regardless of whether you are happy with who won the election or whether you are still angry about whom you think should have been the President, it was a terrible experience for the country which should not happen again. The American people should not have to put up with these kinds of problems. There should be no recounts or hanging chads to deal with. The people should be the sole deciders of who gets to become the President. For us to be able to prevent situations like what happened in the year 2000 or in the prior times in American history would be great reasons alone to do away with the Electoral College. It makes the American people uncomfortable that they may not get their way in deciding who becomes the President. America has a strong democratic tradition that the Electoral College is at odds with. It offends American sensibilities that an unelected institution that the people have no control over can overrule the people. Even though the Electoral College is no organization or body of people that can overrule the peoples will, it has had a similar effect to that in at least three presidential elections so far. There may be plenty more times that this happens in the future if we do not get rid of the Electoral College.

The Electoral College is an out of date system that is not necessary today. Since the popular vote was not counted originally and the states demanded an equal representation in order to enter the union, the Electoral College served its purpose. It allowed the United States to become a country and fortunately it has rarely decided the results of Presidential elections. There are no real legitimate reasons for keeping the Electoral College. The people who live in the small number of states that get to decide who the President is would want to continue having the Electoral College. The average person in most of the country would want to get rid of the Electoral College. The system is not necessary anymore and the people should get to decide who is going to be President. In order to make America into a democracy, the Electoral College should be done away with. By definition a democracy means that the majority rules or that the people decide, the Electoral College takes that power away from the people and gives it to the states. In most cases it is the federal government that has a tremendous amount of power. By getting rid of the Senate, having a direct democracy, electing members of the Federal Courts, among other changes would bring power from the federal government and give it to the people.

While getting rid of the Electoral College would take power away from the swing states and give it to the average person. The power is disproportionally given to the swing voters in the swing states. Instead this power should be more evenly distributed between the American people. One group of people should not have more power than another group of people in deciding who gets to become the President.

Getting rid of the Electoral College would create a national campaign for president. Candidates would no longer have to focus on the swing voters in a small group of states. Presidential candidates would be free to go to all of the states. They would be free to discuss national issues and make the election more about national issues that affect all Americans. Today, the swing states have too much influence in determining the issues and the way that Presidential candidates feel about the issues. Since presidential candidates need to win in Iowa and New Hampshire or place well they have to do what they can to appeal to the voters in those states. That comes with being in favor of ethanol subsidies in Iowa, that comes with being more in line with New Hampshire libertarianism. There are other litmus tests that a candidate must pass to have a chance at winning. This dynamic directly affects national policy once a presidential candidate takes office. Anyone seeking the presidential nomination of their party would never publicly challenge the idea that Iowa and New Hampshire should decide first. They would never publicly challenge the widely held views of voters in those two states either. This all acts to constrain our Presidents and the result is a less democratic process with less democratic results. A Presidential candidate should be forced to take their case to the American people as opposed to only several states. A more national campaign for President would do a superior job of representing what the people want. It would make the process of selecting the next President a more democratic process. Since the presidential candidates are running for national office, doesn't a national campaign make more sense?

If America got rid of the Electoral College it would make a third party candidates bid for the Presidency possible. One of the reasons why a third party candidate cannot ever be President is because of the Electoral College. The candidate that wins 270 Electoral College votes becomes the President. The third party candidate is often a spoiler in Presidential elections. They usually end up hurting the Democrat or the Republican in certain states. If the third party candidate is more liberal, that will harm the Democrat. The liberal third party candidate would take votes that would have gone to the Democrat. Because of this, the Democrat would lose swing states like Florida and Ohio that would be very close and where each vote counts. If the liberal third party candidate were really popular, it would cause the Democrat to lose states that usually would go to the Democrat Presidential candidate like Washington or New Jersey. The Republican candidate would not win a majority of the popular vote in those states but would be the candidate that received the most votes. That means the Republican could win with 44% of the vote in a state where 56% of the vote is split between the Democrat and the liberal independent candidate. The opposite situation can happen as well. There can be a conservative third party candidate that can harm the Republican. The Republican loses crucial votes to the third party candidate so he or she ends up losing closely contested swing states. That alone would cost the Republican the presidency. It is possible that there could be a third party candidate who was a moderate that could take votes away from the Democrat and the Republican. That has happened before but they end up hurting one of the other candidates more than the other. Party loyalty also keeps many from supporting third party candidates for President. It is a nearly impossible situation to elect a third party candidate, yet the chief obstacle is the Electoral College.

In 1912 Republican President William Howard Taft was running for re-election. He was elected easily in 1908 because the popular outgoing Republican president Teddy Roosevelt had selected him as his heir apparent. Yet while Taft was President, Roosevelt became increasingly disillusioned with Taft and came to greatly regret his decision to name Taft as his successor. Roosevelt regretted leaving the White House entirely and desperately wanted his old job back. So Roosevelt ran against Taft for the Republican presidential nomination in 1912. Roosevelt came close to defeating Taft, but Taft was re-nominated as the Republican Presidential nominee. Roosevelt formed a third party called the Bull Moose Party and ran for President as an independent. The Democrat candidate that year was New Jersey Governor Woodrow Wilson. Roosevelt was the moderate candidate in the field, while Taft was the conservative and Wilson was the liberal. Taft and Roosevelt ended up splitting the Republican vote in the election, so even though Wilson only received around forty percent of the popular vote, he won 435 electoral college votes and became President. Roosevelt won around twenty seven percent of the popular vote and 88 Electoral College votes. This is an example of when a popular former President like Theodore Roosevelt that was more moderate than Taft and less liberal than Wilson still lost while running as an independent. Teddy Roosevelt was the best independent presidential candidate that you could think of and that candidate still lost resoundingly.

Another prominent example of a third party candidacy was in 1924. Republican President Calvin Coolidge was running for a full term. He was elected vice President in 1920 with Warren Harding who was elected President. President Harding died in 1923 and then Coolidge was sworn in to be President. The Democrat candidate for President in 1924 was John W. Davis. The third party candidate for President was Progressive Party candidate Wisconsin Republican Senator Robert La Follette. Davis campaigned as a conservative democrat who argued for a smaller federal government like president Coolidge, but Coolidge the conservative Republican President was presiding over a strong economy. La Follette campaigned on a liberal platform that advocated for a larger role for the federal government. La Follette and Davis ended up splitting the Democratic vote for President. Calvin Coolidge won the election of 1924 with fifty four percent of the popular vote and 385 Electoral College votes. John Davis won twenty nine percent of the popular vote along with 136 Electoral College votes. While Robert La Follette won around seventeen percent of the popular vote and only carried his home of state of Wisconsin, which was 13 Electoral College votes. This is another forgotten example of how a third party candidate not only did not have any real chance of winning, it changed what could have been a real contest for the Presidency into a huge landslide for President Coolidge who beat Davis by 25 points.

In 1948 there was another prominent example of how a third party candidate can affect a presidential election. Democrat President Harry Truman was running for his own term. President Franklin Roosevelt died in April of 1945. Harry Truman was his Vice President who became President upon Roosevelt's death. The Republican candidate for President in 1948 was New York Governor Thomas E. Dewey. The third party candidate that year was the segregationist candidate Democrat South Carolina Governor Strom Thurmond. The election was supposed to be close and Strom Thurmond made it more difficult for Truman to win. Yet President Truman won the election with about half of the popular vote and with 303 Electoral College votes. Thomas Dewey won forty-five percent of the popular vote and 189 electoral votes. Strom Thurmond won about three percent of the popular vote and won 39 Electoral College votes. Strom Thurmond's candidacy almost cost Harry Truman the election. Southern states used to vote Democrat for president until the late 1960's. Southerners walked out of the Democratic convention because they adopted a civil rights plank in their platform. Thurmond won Louisiana, Mississippi, Alabama and South Carolina. He won these states plus one electoral vote from Tennessee. If Strom Thurmond had not run as a third party candidate, it would have been easier for Truman to win the election.

In 1968 there was another presidential election with a prominent third party candidate running. The Republican candidate for president was former Vice President Richard Nixon. The Democratic candidate for president was current Vice President Hubert Humphrey. The third party candidate was Alabama Governor George Wallace. Even though Wallace was a Democrat he ran for President as an independent to fight in favor of segregation. This is an instance when a third party candidate cost the Democratic nominee the election. Wallace carried five southern states that totaled 46 Electoral

College votes. These electoral votes traditionally would have gone to the Democratic candidate for President. Wallace also carried around fourteen percent of the popular vote. Richard Nixon won the election with around forty-four percent of the popular vote and 301 Electoral College votes. Humphrey came close to winning but won around forty-two percent of the popular vote and won 191 Electoral College votes. This was another election where there was a prominent third party candidate who potentially affected the outcome of the election.

In 1980 there was a less prominent example of a third party candidate affecting the elections outcome. The Democratic candidate for President was President Jimmy Carter. The Republican candidate for president was former California Governor Ronald Reagan. The third party candidate was Independent candidate John B. Anderson who was a Republican congressman from Illinois. Ronald Reagan won the election in a landslide with fifty-one percent of the popular vote and 489 Electoral College votes. President Jimmy Carter won around forty percent of the popular vote and 49 Electoral College votes. John B. Anderson won around nine percent of the popular vote and no Electoral College votes. Anderson did not affect the outcome of the election, yet he took many votes from Ronald Reagan as he campaigned as a moderate third choice.

After 1912, one of the most prominent examples of a third party candidate affecting the outcome of a presidential election was in 1992. The Republican candidate was President George H.W. Bush. The Democratic candidate for president was Arkansas Governor Bill Clinton. The third party candidate was Texas billionaire Ross Perot. Perot ran to the right of President Bush and attracted many conservative voters who became disillusioned with his presidency. Bill Clinton won the election with forty-two percent of the vote and 370 Electoral College votes. President Bush came in second winning around thirty-nine percent of the popular vote and 168 Electoral College votes. Ross Perot won around nineteen percent of the popular vote and no electoral votes. Ross Perot won the second largest percent of the popular vote in American history for a third party candidate. That was more than any third party candidate has ever won besides Teddy Roosevelt in 1912. It's quite possible that if Perot were not in the race that President Bush would have been re-elected. His presence certainly was responsible for Bill Clintons lopsided Electoral College win.

In 1996 Ross Perot ran for President again as a third party candidate. President Clinton was running for re-election and Kansas Republican Senator Bob Dole became the nominee for the Republican Party. Perot seemed to have hurt the Republican and helped Bill Clinton again. Perot ran a more conservative campaign than Senator Dole and took more votes away from the Republican. President Clinton was re-elected with around forty-eight percent of the popular vote and with 379 Electoral College votes. Bob Dole won forty-four percent of the popular vote and 159 Electoral College votes. Ross Perot won seven percent of the popular vote and no Electoral College votes. In a case like this, the third party candidate not only cost Dole millions of votes, but also less obvious is that he cost Dole many Electoral College votes as well. The votes that went to Perot were in many traditionally Republican states that went to Perot to deny Dole a majority. So these electoral votes went to Clinton instead of going to Dole in many states. Ross Perot is a prominent third party candidate who had no real chance of winning the Presidency, yet tilted the outcome of two elections in a row in the favor of the Democratic candidate, Bill Clinton.

The last prominent example of a third party candidate skewing presidential election results was in the year 2000. This was a particularly bitter experience for people, especially if you are a Democrat. The election was a very close election. The Democratic candidate was Vice President Al Gore. The Republican candidate for president was Texas Governor George W. Bush. The most prominent independent candidate was Green party candidate consumer advocate Ralph Nader. George W. Bush won the election with forty-eight percent of the popular vote and 271 Electoral College votes. Al

Gore lost narrowly with around forty-eight percent of the popular vote and 266 Electoral College votes. Ralph Nader won around three percent of the popular vote and no Electoral College votes. Al Gore beat George W. Bush by half a million votes in the popular vote but lost the Electoral College. The three percent of the popular vote that went to Nader would have gone to Gore. Nader ran far to the left of Gore who ran as a moderate Democrat. This is another situation when a third party candidate changed the results of the election. In many states the election results were very close and took a long time to determine the winner of the state. Yet it was the state of Florida, which would be the decider in that year. There were only hundreds of votes in difference between Bush and Gore. Over a month of recounts ensued. The Gore and Bush campaigns decided the difference in the Supreme Court in December of 2000. The court voted 5-4 that the Gore campaign could not continue with recounts so the election went to Bush. Bush carried Florida by some 500 votes. There were many reported problems with ballots and voting irregularities. The election results were so close between Bush and Gore that Nader made a difference in the outcome, even though he only won around three percent of the vote. The American people had to put up with recalls and court battles and a lot of partisan wrangling before the election results could be determined. Not only that, but the American people had decided on one person being President and the Electoral College had decided on another candidate. This happened twice before in 1876 and 1888, it was the only time it had happened since then. The Electoral College should not reign supreme over the American people. Obviously Republicans are happy with this result in 2000 and the Democrats are upset, the reverse situation could easily happen in the future. Regardless, the American people should be the sole deciders of presidential elections, not the Electoral College. This is the most prominent and controversial example of late that shows how the Electoral College can get in the way of the people.

There have been times that a third party candidate helped the Republican. There are times that the third party candidate helped the Democrat. There have been more times when the third party candidate or candidates have not made any difference. In 1980 John B. Anderson had a more benign affect on the elections outcome when Ronald Reagan won in a large landslide anyway. In 2000 it was a particularly controversial and close election that Nader had an affect on the outcome. There should be third party candidates for President. The point of learning about these past election outcomes is to emphasize that third party candidates have no chance of getting elected President with the Electoral College in place. They typically benefit one candidate at the expense of the other. It would still be a difficult upward climb to elect a third party candidate president without the Electoral College. Yet it would actually be possible for one to win without the Electoral College.

The Electoral College should not be able to supersede the will of the voters. When there is a close election when a candidate could win the Electoral College and lose the popular vote and still win the election it is a wrong situation. To make America more democratic we should get rid of the Electoral College and make each vote count. The Electoral College makes some states matter more than others during the political primaries and the general election. The swing states are given plenty of attention while the rest of the states are ignored. If there was no Electoral College then we could have national primaries and not put so much emphasis on a select few of the states. The people should be given the ability to make decisions for the presidency. All of the people deserve to be courted for their votes. People in all of the states should be solicited by the presidential candidates for their support. The interests of all of the people and all of the states should be represented equally in political primaries and the general election for President.

There are some potential problems that could arise out of getting rid of the Electoral College. There are also some potential problems with getting rid of the early state primary system and having a national primary. If we got rid of the Electoral College, there could be too much attention paid to people in the most populous states like California, Texas, Florida, New York and other large states. Small states like Alaska, Wyoming, North Dakota and others would be ignored. This is a valid concern. Yet at the end of the day, since a state has more people that doesn't mean it's a bad thing to pay more attention to people who live in those states. There would also be a partisan component to how presidential candidates campaigned for president. A Republican candidate would not spend a bunch of time campaigning in Massachusetts or New York City. Just as a Democrat candidate would not spend a lot of time in Dallas or North Dakota. The Republican or Democrat would campaign aggressively to increase the turnout for the members of their party nationwide. More than likely what would happen if they removed the Electoral College is that you would see Republican and Democrat presidential candidates campaigning heavily in different states. Because the name of the game is turn out. If the Democrats have higher voter turnout from their base than Republicans then they will win the Presidency. The opposite situation is true. Even though they would fight for swing voters, swing voters only represent around 10% of the electorate. These are people that would truly be open to voting for a Democrat or a Republican for President. Around 45% of the people would only vote Republican and around 45% of the people would only vote Democrat. The 45% of the voting population is a far larger number of people than 10%. Pumping up turnout from the base is crucial in order to win the Presidency in the 21st century. Not to mention, a candidate could get the true believers to show up at the polls and vote. Swing voters on the other hand may not be as interested in voting or showing up to vote. So its not just about sheer numbers, it is also about who is most likely to show up on Election Day and vote for you.

Would the swing states all of the sudden become irrelevant? Yes and no. States like Ohio, Michigan, Florida, North Carolina, Virginia, and Pennsylvania would still see a lot of activity from presidential candidates. These are states with large populations and relatively even numbers of Republican and Democrat voters, this would still attract candidates running for president. There would be smaller swing states that would suffer. States like Iowa, New Hampshire, Nevada and New Mexico would suffer as a result. It's not that the presidential candidates would not court the voters in those states. First of all, the voters in these states are pretty evenly split between the Republicans and the Democrats. This would be reason enough to attract presidential candidates to campaign in these states. Secondly, since getting rid of the Electoral College would create a national election, candidates would be under considerable pressure to campaign in all fifty states. There would only be so much time that a candidate could spend in each state. The states that they would visit most often would depend on their strategy for winning the election. If they were a Republican who just wanted to maximize voter turnout they would visit primarily southern states, Midwestern states and half of the west. If a Democrat were doing something similar they would primarily campaign in the northeast, west coast and along with the upper Midwest. There could be a third party candidate that campaigned for a more centrist direction that would attract people from all over the country. Getting rid of the Electoral College would allow presidential candidates more flexibility in determining what states they could campaign in. They would be free to employ whatever strategy that they wanted in order to get elected. The candidates would be able to fight for every vote and take their campaigns all over America instead of the select swing states. In the current process it is all about locking down red and blue states and doing whatever it takes to win the swing states. This current strategy would no longer be necessary if the Electoral College were done away with.

The next potential problem with getting rid of the Electoral College is that it would weaken the states. The Electoral College was created to give the states a say in who became President. Since the popular vote for President was counted in 1824, the Electoral College did not serve much purpose any longer. The electoral college and the fact that a candidate needed a certain number of electoral college votes in order to win caused the states to experience more power than they would have otherwise. Presidential candidates needed to make promises to states and campaign directly for states support. However these days there a small group of states that receive a lot of attention while most states don't receive any. The Electoral College actually causes states to be worse off. Sure there are some swing states that benefit from the increased attention and the fact that presidents have to do certain things that benefit those states in order to win and get reelected. Yet most states suffer because they don't get any attention while some swing states have too much control over the President and their policies. The power of some swing states even stifles politicians that want to become President in the future. They are afraid of challenging things too much and don't want to ruin their chances of ever becoming President. If the Electoral College were done away with, the states would be on a more equal footing than they are now. Ultimately getting rid of the electoral college is not necessarily about making the states more powerful or equally represented, its about making America into a democracy by assuring that the candidate who wins the most votes wins the election for President.

Another potential problem with getting rid of the Electoral College would be that candidates would only focus on the large cities. If they did not have to focus on states for Electoral College votes they would be free to go to New York City or Los Angeles only. Since most people are located in cities wouldn't it make the most sense to campaign in urban areas? That is a potential problem but first of all, getting rid of the Electoral College would mean that the popular vote is what counted. The current system is unfair because presidential candidates aren't forced to campaign where most people in the country are like California, Texas, New York, Georgia, and Illinois etc. It would only be a more democratic process if the people were served better. The second thing is that getting rid of the Electoral College would not necessarily make the large cities so important there would still be the issue of voter turnout. A Democratic candidate would go to places like Los Angeles, Chicago and New York City to pump up party turnout. Most people in those cities as well as other urban areas tend to be more Democrat. Where the Republican candidate would be more likely to visit rural states, rural areas of large states and exurbs. Those areas tend to be more Republican so they would need to go there to drive up voter turnout for their party. Suburbs and swing states like Ohio, Florida, Pennsylvania, Virginia and Michigan would still be coveted because they are areas with large populations and relatively even numbers of Republicans and Democrats. That's where the elections are won and lost usually. Getting rid of the Electoral College would not unfairly give urban areas more attention. It's unfair how little attention voters in urban areas get currently, getting rid of the Electoral College would make things fairer for everyone.

There are people that feel that the Electoral College maintains the federal character of America. The Electoral College keeps the federalist tradition alive and forces presidential candidates to pay attention to states with smaller populations. The Electoral College only causes the presidential candidates to focus on a small number of states. Some of the swing states like New Hampshire, Nevada and Iowa have smaller populations, but most swing states have larger populations like Florida, Arizona, Ohio, Pennsylvania, Virginia, North Carolina and Indiana. While there are small states like Vermont, Hawaii, Wyoming and Alaska that receive no attention. So the Electoral College does not force the candidates to visit or pay attention to the smaller states, it only forces them to focus their campaigns on the swing states. Not to mention, the Electoral College only endorses the tradition that the states or in some situations that the Congress decide the outcome of a presidential election. Getting rid of the Electoral College and replacing it with a popular vote would make America more democratic and better serve the American people. Regardless of where someone lives, making the popular vote count would give all Americans more power and would encourage more Americans to turnout and vote for President. It's unfair that the swing states dominate the candidates attention and the people should be able to decide who their President is, not the states or the Congress.

Is it unfair that the members of all political parties must choose their nominee on the same day? Can the government dictate that political parties must hold their nomination on the same day? Political parties may decide how they would like their own party's nomination process to go and they are the ultimate deciders in how they run their own parties primary. It very well may not be possible to get all political parties to agree to hold their presidential primary on the same day. It may not be possible to convince one political party to do this at all. The government could not force political parties to hold their primary on the same day either. The government could not tell all political parties to hold a national primary on the same day either. There would be issues with all fifty states plus territories holding a primary on the same day. It would be an expensive endeavor to coordinate and its not clear that the federal government would be allowed to force a national primary on the same day onto the states and territories. The idea of having political parties hold their primary for the presidency on the same day is a suggestion. It would be a way for more people in a political party to have a say in who becomes their nominee. It would be a way for more candidates to have an opportunity to become their party's nominee. It would make the nominating process fairer to the candidates and to the voters. It would also prevent early states from getting a disproportionate amount of attention, while most states are ignored. It would be a step in making America more democratic.

Wouldn't a national primary on the same day hurt the interests of the voters? Would it give Americans too little time to get to know the candidates running for president for their political party? That certainly is a concern that with a quick national primary that the people would not have enough time to assess the candidates. There is the possibility that there would not be enough time to assess the candidates because most people don't start paying attention until the primaries. The way the Republican and Democratic primaries go today is that the vast majority of the people have no control over who becomes the presidential nominee for their party. They may have a lot of extra time to think about whom they would vote for if their state primary happens months later than Iowa's does. But it does not give any of the people a real choice. In most instances, the person that you wanted to vote for didn't do well in the first several states like Iowa, New Hampshire and South Caroline and dropped out of the race by the time that you get to vote. In most cases, whoever wins the first several primaries wins the presidential nomination and all other opponents are forced to withdraw from the race due to lack of money and support. Everyone likes to support a winner. If we had a national primary on the same day, it would give the candidates running for President an equal opportunity to win their political parties nomination for President.

Even though having a national primary on the same day may give other candidates a good chance at winning the nomination who ordinarily would not be able to win, wouldn't a national primary disqualify the type of candidates who could win the nomination now? There would be a possibility that there would be candidates that could be uncompetitive if there were a national primary on the same day. A national primary would require all candidates to appeal to the members of their party throughout the country. Most members of political parties generally have the same political views regardless of where they live in the country. Republicans, Democrats, Libertarians, Greens, etc generally have the same views as others members of their political party. It could be possible for any person to become the nominee if there were a national primary on the same day. A national primary very well may not make it less likely for candidates to win their parties nomination; it could make it more likely for other types of candidates to win the nomination. It could give all candidates an equal chance of winning their parties nomination for President. Under the current system, most people running for their party's nomination are forced to drop out of the race if they lost the first couple of primaries. There are a lot of people who drop out even before the first primary vote is counted. A national primary on the same day would give each candidate an equal chance of getting nominated, it would be fair to all members of the nations political parties to get to choose their nominee, and other nominees that would never have any chance of winning their political parties nomination under the current system would have a chance.

Political parties should be forced to hold their primaries for President on the same day across the country. As it goes currently, Iowa is the first caucus state that gets to decide who becomes President. Whether it's for the Democrats or the Republicans, Iowa voters are the first that get to decide who becomes President. After Iowa, New Hampshire voters get to vote. The third state is South Carolina. All fifty states and territories get to vote in political party primaries. Iowa votes in February and the last states usually vote in June. It's not fair that voters in Iowa get to decide who becomes the presidential nominee for each party. Usually there are around a dozen people or so running for President in each party. After Iowa many decide to drop out due to poor performance in the primary. The candidate that wins usually starts building unstoppable momentum into New Hampshire, South Carolina and so on until they are the only candidate left in the primary. All state primaries for President should take place on the same day. All voters throughout the country should have an equal chance of getting to decide who the nominee for their party is. It would be fairer to the voters and to the candidates running. It would give more candidates a chance to win as well.

The country should have national political primaries and no electoral college. Smaller states that are the first states that vote in political primaries have too much power. Some of those states are also swing states in the general election for President. If the country had a national primary on the same day, that would allow a greater variety of people to become the nominee for president. This would result in a greater variety of candidates that could become President. The Electoral College causes the candidates for president to focus too much on a select group of states. The candidates for president should campaign all across the country. The Electoral College should never overrule the rule of the people as it has in three presidential elections so far. If there were no electoral college then it would be possible for a third party candidate to get elected president. Overall, the American people should get to decide who the president is and there should be nobody or group of people who have more power than the American people. In order to make America into a democracy, the Electoral College has to go. National primaries would make the presidential nomination process more democratic as well. In the next chapter I will talk about why we should increase the number of representatives in the House of Representatives and why state legislatures and governors should not be in charge of redistricting.

# Chapter Eight

The next step in the process of making America into a democracy would be to increase the number of representatives in the House of Representatives. Another step would be to change the way that redistricting is done. These two issues are related because the state legislature and Governor create the congressional districts, which will determine what political party can win that district. If the number of representatives is increased then it will give those politicians even greater power in deciding what party will win those congressional seats. There is an obvious conflict of interest having the state legislature and governor decide redistricting. Not to mention, many congressional districts do a poor job of representing the people that live there. It would be more democratic if a non-partisan group created the congressional districts and if there were more representatives in the House. This would permit the people to be better represented and better served in Washington. These changes would cause people to be better represented and better served in their own state capitals. Making the House of Representatives and the state houses more responsive to the people would make America more democratic and the people would have more control over their own government. Political parties, politicians, special interests, corporations and lobbyists would lose power with these changes implemented while the people would gain power.

We should increase the number of representatives in the House of Representatives. There are 435 members in the House, this has remained the same for decades. An act of Congress in 1911 set the number of Representatives by law at 435 members. Each member of the House should represent a similar number of people. Increasing the number of representatives in the House would more equally represent the American people. It would become more democratic if each member of the House represented a similar number of people. Having more representatives would better represent the American people. The state legislature and governor should not be able to decide the congressional districts. They use the power of their office to advance their partisan interests. They are doing what is best for their party and not what is best for the people who live in their state. There are many congressional districts that are created to give either political party control over the district.

The House of Representatives was created out of a compromise when the constitution was created during the constitutional convention in 1787. Part of the compromise was the US Senate, which was created to give all of the states equal representation in the Congress. While the House of Representatives was created to give equal representation to the American people. Even though every state was given a representative in the House, a state was given additional members if their states population was larger. The more people that lived in a state, the larger the number of representatives the state would have. Each member of the House represents a congressional district. In a state like Wyoming, the entire state is a congressional district because Wyoming only has one member of the House of Representatives. Whereas a state like California has fifty-three congressional districts. Each congressional district is essentially the size of a county. The states legislature and governor get to decide the boundaries of each congressional district.

The congressional districts have changed over time and lately; they have tended to coincide with the party that is in control of the state legislature and the Governors mansion. Republican state governments draw congressional districts that will give their fellow Republicans the best chance of winning those seats. While the Democrat state governments draw congressional districts that will give their fellow Democrats the best chance of getting elected to Congress. The process of creating congressional districts is way too partisan. It helps political parties hold onto power and keep the members of the their party in charge. Most congressional districts are created so a majority of the people who vote in the district are a Republican or a Democrat. If most of the people who live in a congressional district are a Democrat, it will be easy for a Democrat candidate to get elected and to continue getting re-elected. If most of the people who live in a congressional district are Republican, then it will be easy for a Republican candidate to win and keep getting re-elected. A vast majority of the countries congressional districts have been designed this way by the states legislatures.

Since most congressional districts are created to give an advantage to either party, these are not districts that are created to benefit the people who live in them. This represents something called gerrymandering. This is the process of creating in some cases, odd-looking congressional districts on a map. These districts are meant to maximize the political advantage of either party. The term gerrymandering comes from the Boston Gazette in 1812. This was in reaction to the Massachusetts Governor Elbridge Gerry creating state senate districts that benefitted his party. Some of the districts were so obscene that one of the districts around Boston looked like a salamander. So the words Gerry and salamander were put together to create the word gerrymander. This word forever represented artificially created districts that benefit one particular political party or another. It's a tool of those in charge of the state to help those in their party gain additional power and hold onto that power. The political party that has a large majority in the state legislature and usually holds the governor's mansion creates state and congressional districts that benefits their political party. This is something that happens in a vast majority of states in the country. There are a small group of swing states where some years the Democrats run the governors mansion and the legislature. There are other times that the governor's mansions and the legislature are run by the Republicans. In these states there is a kind of on and off gerrymandering that rotates between each political party. All the while the people who live in each state are ignored and are unable to do anything about this.

There are very few congressional districts where there are more independent voters or where the district is not politically safe for a Republican or a Democrat. These are the so-called swing districts, these congressional districts are politically competitive. The politicians who become the congressman or congresswoman of the district has to be careful to appeal to those in both parties. Since there are very few of these kind of congressional districts, it is rare to have people in congress that are moderate. The other problem is that when one party that has a majority in Congress is unpopular, the members of that party that are serving in a swing district are the most likely to lose their seat. This makes it very difficult for members of swing districts to stay in their seats for very long. The other problem is that some of these people serving in congress become arrogant or too partisan and side with their own party too much. That sometimes ends up alienating the majority of voters in their district who are not members of the congressman's or congresswomen's political party. That can also lead to those members of the congress losing their seat. The politician that becomes the congressman or congresswoman of a swing district doe not survive in office nearly as long as members of the congress that are serving in gerrymandered congressional districts. This is a big reason why the Congress is so partisan and gridlocked. That's a big reason why members of the congress are protected with gerrymandered districts. It helps them and the party that runs their state legislature wants to further the interests of their party. In exchange the members of the state government ask those serving in congress to vote in a way that benefits their state. The members of the state government also hope to become members of the Congress someday and they hope to have a politically safe seat so they can serve for decades and become wealthy and powerful in Washington.

There should be a non-partisan group of people who get to create congressional districts and state districts. The districts should either be arbitrary and be made to last or they should be made by a non-partisan group of people. Since it may be impossible to have a truly non-partisan panel of people deciding, the people should have the ultimate say over the congressional and state boundaries. They are the ones who live there after all. It should be up to the people who live there who end up making these decisions. The people should be able to present proposed congressional and state districts to the voters and ask for the voter's approval. This will not eliminate partisanship from politics much less from the re-districting process. But at least the people would get to decide what the boundaries are for congressional districts and state districts instead of the current political party in power. The party in power that carves up districts to support those in their party and to expand their power and influence. The people are the ones that are supposed to be represented, not the political parties, politicians, and the special interest groups that have a vested interest in their political party staying in charge.

The people could present proposals for what the congressional districts and state districts would look like. The proposals that garnered enough signatures would be on the ballot. The people in each state would get to decide on what the congressional districts would be in their own state. People would not be allowed to decide what the congressional and state districts would look like in other states. This would help make districts that would be more to the peoples liking instead of those serving in the legislature and governors mansion. There would still be partisan or politically safe districts, yet at least the people would be in a position to decide what the districts would look like. If they didn't feel like a particular arrangement was working out they could change it. It is better than leaving it up to the politicians in power to decide what their own districts look like. There would be plenty of independent voters who would get to have input in creating the districts instead of politicians that are creating districts that are for the maximum benefit of their own party. There would be more transparency and the districts at the state and congressional level would become more politically competitive. More politically competitive districts would benefit the people and better serve the people who are not members of either political party. More politically competitive districts would force the politicians to become more beholden to those that they represent.

If there were more congressional districts the people would be better represented. At the moment there are congressional districts of all different sizes and populations. The district with the smallest number of people is the 1st district of Rhode Island with around half a million people in the district. There are other congressional districts that are an entire state like Montana. Montana has the largest number of people in their congressional district at one million people. The average congressional district has around 700,000 people. The congressional districts throughout the country are very different from each other. The physical size of the district or its location is not as important as how many people are in each district. Is it really fair that there are districts with as little as 500,000 people and there are districts with a million people? Just because of where you live directly influences your representation in Congress. There are over three hundred million Americans so congressional districts will have to hold many people. There could be a goal of adding additional members to the House of Representatives so that the people could be represented more equally.

The country has had 435 members in the House of Representatives and six non-voting members (who can vote in committees but not on the floor, but they should be allowed too) for over one hundred years. This is in spite of the fact that the country has three times as many people as we had one hundred years ago. Adding representatives and creating more congressional districts is not only fairer to each voter, it would make the Congress more democratic. There would be more people fighting for the interests and ideas of more Americans. It would help localize congressmen that get spread too thin amongst too large a congressional district. If there were no United States Senate anymore all of the sudden there would be 100 politicians looking for a new job anyway, why not create some space in the House for them?

Adding additional representatives in the House would make the members of the Congress less powerful. It would dilute the power that the current members of the House of Representatives have. This would be better because it should be less about power for members of Congress and more about representing their constituents. Some members of Congress are there for decades and have powerful committee positions. These congressmen collect many supporters and increase their influence in Washington as their tenures continue. There are plenty of special interest groups that give money to Democrats or give money to Republicans. There are also many corporations and special interest groups that give money to Republicans and to Democrats in Congress. If there are more members in the House of Representatives, it makes influencing a member of Congress less valuable and all the more difficult. It would require more resources from corporations and special interest groups to influence enough members of Congress to further their agenda. This would make it more difficult for these groups to have a lot of influence in Washington. It would also make the individual members of Congress less powerful and influential. Having additional members of the House of Representatives would increase attention on constituents. It would be easier for a member of Congress to represent the interests of one hundred thousand people than it would be for a congressman to represent the more varied interests of one million people. Increasing the number of representatives in the House would increase the power of the American voter, while reducing the power of the Congressman and the special interests. That would make America more democratic and would help clean up politics in Washington.

The House of Representatives is supposed to represent the will of the people in Congress. While the Senate is supposed to represent the states equally and cool the populist enthusiasm in the House. If there was no Senate and the House of Representatives had a larger number of representatives, the Congress would be more democratic. It would more accurately reflect the interests and the will of the American people. This would be a lot more democratic than the current situation is. The members of the Congress would also be a lot less powerful. It would be a lot more difficult for special interests and corporations to influence the Congress. Senators individually are quite powerful. Yet if there was no Senate and the House had a larger number of representatives this would make each individual member serving in the House of Representatives less powerful. Special interests and corporations would have a lot more difficulty in influencing a far larger group of politicians that have less power. It would not be worth that much to influence a couple dozen members of the House. It would require influencing a majority of the members of the House. This would require a lot more money and resources than it would to influence the people serving in the House and Senate now. Since the representatives in the House would be representing smaller congressional districts, they would be more beholden to those in their district. There would be a larger level of scrutiny and the members of Congress would better represent the people who live in their district.

Exactly how many additional seats in the House of Representatives should be added? There would have to be around one thousand people serving in the House in order to make representation similar to how it was decades ago. They would need to triple the number of representatives to bring representation back to where it was one hundred years ago when Congress fixed the number of representatives at 435 members. The state of New Hampshire has around one million people yet they have 400 representatives in their state house. Having far higher rates of representation than Congress is hardly unprecedented in the United States. Since there would be no Electoral College anymore (See Chapter 7) then it would not matter if a state with a large population received additional members of congress. The states with a larger population would receive additional members of the House in order to equally represent the people in America. Montana would have to receive another representative given that they have the most people in their congressional district. It would not happen in order to make some states even more powerful than other states. The intended effect is to empower the people and create additional representatives that will be more responsive to their constituents. It is about reducing the number of people represented in an average district. If the average congressional district has

700,000 people and there are 435 members of the House, then if you triple the number of representatives the average district would have around 230,000 people instead. This may not seem like an important difference but it's about two things. It's not just about increasing representation for the people and making politicians more responsive to them; it's also about reducing the power that politicians in the Congress have. It's simple division, power is in the numerator and the number of representatives is in the denominator. Increasing the denominator will reduce the numerator; it means less power for the average member of Congress. It is about giving the people more of a say in how their federal government is run. It is supposed to dilute the power of the politicians, the special interest groups, the political parties and all other sources of power and influence that can get in the way of what the American people want. This is principally about taking power out of Washington and putting it into the hands of the voters throughout the country. This is about decentralizing power that has become far to centralized in Washington.

Some may worry about large states getting all of the influence when those states have a lot of representatives in Congress and the small states have very few. That is an entirely legitimate concern. Yet the country is increasingly being met with issues that are national in scope. The issues of taxes and spending in the federal government, climate change, social security, federal regulations, national defense, Medicare, terrorism, government programs, etc are all federal issues that must be dealt with by a national consensus. Large states would not be able to take all of the attention with legislation. There are forty-nine other states that would object to one state getting special treatment. Not to mention, the representatives could always attach bills to larger must pass bills that would directly benefit their state. This is something that always happens now and has always happened in the past. Whether people think it is right or not, it's how business is done in Washington and the members of congress are under constant pressure to deliver for the constituents in their state.

Some people may worry about the people having too much influence over the House of Representatives. They may worry that the House becomes too populist and makes decisions that are more rash and less thought out. There is no such a thing as the people having too much influence over the House of Representatives. Especially in a time when the members of Congress have way too much power and the people are not represented well in Washington. Not to mention, it is a completely reasonable request that there are additional members in the House of Representatives. Considering the fact that the population has increased by around two hundred million people since the last time that the number of representatives was permitted to increase. If you believe that the House of Representatives would become too populist with having additional representatives, then you thought that it was too populist in the past. Having additional members of the House would not only keep up with population growth in the country, it would also make the federal government more democratic. It would put more power in the hands of the voters than in the hands of politicians. It would mean additional representatives representing more of the diversity and different priorities of the American people. It would assure that the people and society overall was more equally and accurately represented in Washington. That by definition would be a more democratic and responsive House of Representatives.

If we increased the number of representatives in the House, some may worry that the House of Representatives would become too populist. That the members may work too hard to please their voters and do what's politically expedient. It may give the politicians a lot less flexibility in doing things that are good for the country yet are not popular. This is a possibility, but the people seem to have a good intuition for what is good for the nation and what makes good public policy. It would not be a big problem if the members of the Congress were more responsive to their constituents. Even if there were additional members in the House of Representatives it wouldn't mean that the people would have more power automatically. There would be more equitable representation but political parties, politicians, corporations, special interest groups would still have the most power in dictating legislation in

Congress. Adding additional representatives in Congress would help restore the balance in favor of the people and away from the entrenched interests in Washington. The idea that the Congress would become too populist is not realistic given the power of various groups in the Capital. If the House of Representatives did a better job at representing the people, their approval rating would be considerably higher than it is today. As of this writing it is around ten percent, which is a record low approval rating for the Congress by the public.

Some may be against adding members to the House of Representatives because they don't like Congressmen already, why add more? Why create a larger group of unpopular people? The Congress is certainly unpopular and the average person does not like politicians, much less members of Congress. The idea of adding representatives to the House is to better serve the American people. A larger number of people serving in the House would mean more representatives representing fewer people on average. That would make it easier for them to represent their congressional districts constituents. It would also make each member more responsive to the demands of the people they represent. More members in the House of Representatives would be more democratic. Adding additional members to the House of Representatives would also create an opportunity to make each congressional district have roughly the same number of people. It's not fair that your representation in the House of Representatives is based solely off of where you happen to live. Adding additional members would certainly create more Congressmen, but it would also reduce the power of the current members. The larger the number of Congressmen, the less power each individual member of the Congress has. That is less influence which makes it more expensive for special interests to influence members of the Congress and it spreads out the level of power that each Congressmen would have. Less powerful congressmen and less powerful special interests would give more power to the American people and less to these sources of power in Washington that have far too much power.

Would adding additional members to the House of Representatives make some states over represented in Congress? The people would be more equally represented, but wouldn't the states become very unequally represented? There is a concern that the states would become quite unequal if some states had many representatives in Congress and other states only had one. This concern was addressed initially by creating the United States Senate. Each state received two senators. If the people decided to keep the Senate around, then this would assure that the states would be equally represented and that the people were equally represented as well. If the Senate were done away with and there was only a House of Representatives, then there could be a real issue of some states having little influence while other states have way too much power in Washington. At the end of the day, making the country more democratic does mean that the federal government as well as the states lose power and that power goes to the people. In order to address the concerns of the states, the people would have the power to give the states more power. The people would be able to vote on matters that could give the federal government more or less power. They would also have the same ability to give the states more or less power. There could be another compromise reached that would respect the sovereignty of the states and the federalist tradition of the country. With a constitutional convention the states could demand that another amendment to the Constitution is added to help retain the influence and power for the states in the event that the people decided to get rid of the United States Senate.

Would we have to keep adding additional members to the House of Representatives as the population continued to get larger? We would not necessarily have to keep adding additional members of Congress every time the population increased by some percentage or millions of people. The population of the country may well stay the same in the future or decline. If our population rose rapidly it would not necessarily be a problem to increase the number of representatives in the House. It may seem ridiculous to have thousands of people serving in the House, yet it would make representation more equal and better serve the American people. If the population rose so much that we had thousands of representatives that may or may not be a good thing. Yet in principle, the point of increasing the number of representatives in the House is to keep representation as equal as possible amongst the congressional districts and to make the Congress and the country more democratic. Adding members to the House would make it so the ever-increasing population could be represented more equally. The larger the numbers of members in the Congress, the less power each individual member of Congress would have. It may sound counter intuitive to say that more members in the Congress would make Congress weaker, but it would give the people more power. Even though the individual members would have less power, they would be more beholden to the people and the increased number of representatives would dilute the power of other special interests, it would increase representation for the people. There would be more people fighting for the interests of the people. More Congressmen serving a smaller number of people each would make each member more responsive and more interested in representing their constituents.

The governors and state legislators should not be able to create congressional districts. They should not be able to create state legislative districts either. It could be difficult to create, but there should be a truly nonpartisan committee of people that create the states congressional districts and the legislative districts. The voters of each state should have some kind of final approval over the committee's recommendations. To make things more democratic the people should have the final say over what the congressional and legislative districts look like. If the Governor and the majority of the members serving in the state legislature are of one party, they will use their power to create legislative and congressional districts that are the most beneficial to their political party. This helps politicians create so-called "safe districts" where a majority of the voters in the district are registered members of their party. That creates politicians that are more partisan, less responsive to their constituents and become permanent career politicians that get captured by special interest groups. The people have no ability to get rid of these kinds of politicians. If the legislative and congressional districts were competitive and not created by the very politicians that ran in them, the process would be more democratic and transparent.

Wouldn't taking the redistricting decision out of politicians hands have unforeseen consequences? Is it possible that some negative consequences could come? It may be difficult to find a non-partisan group of people that could be trusted to make decisions. Redistricting could also lead to a more partisan make-up of congressional districts and legislative districts. The change of allowing a non-partisan committee to decide what congressional districts and legislative districts look like would not be perfect. But it would be better than allowing the Governor and the legislators to decide. The decision should be taken out of the hands of politicians and in the hands of a committee of non-partisan people. The public would be able to approve or disapprove their final decision. Or the voters themselves could propose what the state and congressional districts looked like and the competing proposals could go before the voters. The proposal that received the highest number of votes would become law. This could happen whenever there is a statewide election; in the status quo redistricting can only happen every ten years after the census takes place.

Would a "non-partisan" committee be truly non-partisan? It could be difficult to locate a committee of people that are truly non-partisan. Not to mention, who would decide who sat on the committee? Would the legislature and governor get to decide? Or would the people get to decide? The people should be able to decide who resided on the committee. There would still be a conflict of interest problem with not allowing the Governor and Legislature to create the districts, yet allowing them to decide who gets to sit on some supposedly non-partisan committee. The people should get to decide who sits on the committee. There should be an odd number of people who sit on the committee. There could be five people who serve. The people who run could model their behavior off of positions like running for attorney general or public utility commission. The candidates running would have to be non-partisan people that had no affiliation with politicians and political parties.

Is it possible to force all states to adopt a non-partisan committee of people to decide what the state legislative and congressional districts looked like? Would it be possible to do that and force elections to occur to decide what people serve on the board? The federal government would not be allowed to force the states to do this. There would have to be a constitutional amendment to force the states to do so. The most likely way to create a redistricting committee would be for a grass roots effort on the part of citizens in states throughout the country to demand this. The federal government could not force states to adopt committees, but the change could come from the people. It could be difficult to ask state legislators and governors to give up the power that comes with redistricting. There are states that have ballot measure systems and people can propose changes and take the issue to the states voters. Not all states have ballot measure systems, yet it is possible with enough support for things to change in states.

Wouldn't there be a chance that things could become extremely competitive and more partisan if things changed? If a majority of the people lived in a state were members of the same political party, wouldn't they vote to make all districts to the benefit of their party? This could be a genuine possibility in certain states that are very Republican or very Democrat. Yet there are many states that are like that already where the majority of the states residents or either Democrats or Republicans. They elect Republicans or Democrats respectively to their states legislature and to the Governors mansion. Then those people generally get to decide what the states legislative and congressional districts look like. This seems like an unfair process, yet it is standard practice throughout the country. Surely there is a better way. The point of making the country more democratic is to give the people more control over their own government. Taking redistricting out the politicians hands and giving that power to the people would create results that were to the peoples liking. Even if it created a more partisan makeup than exists currently, at least the people would decide. Partisan loyalties change over time and don't last forever. If America became a democracy maybe partisan loyalties would decline because people could decide issues one at a time.

If the majority of the people in a state were members of one political party, wouldn't they vote to create districts that permanently kept their party in power? That is also a very real possibility. If a majority of the people in a state were in one political party, why wouldn't they give their party control over everything? The first thing is that very thing already happens in many states throughout the country already. Secondly, making America more democratic means giving the people more power over how their country and state is run. Others who do not like it have to live with the consequences of a more democratic society. The people must be trusted to make decisions that are the best for their county, state and country. The third thing is that there very well could be a non-partisan committee of people that arbitrarily decide what the states legislative and congressional districts look like. It would be difficult to find a truly non-partisan group of people, yet the framework of a committee could be constructed in such a way that it would result in a non-partisan outcome. The people would get to decide who would be on the committee; maybe the spirit of the committee would be non-partisan. Yet something truly democratic would wield the influence and decisions of the voters. How could it not become a partisan tool for the majority? That seems like a very likely side-affect of a very democratic system. The majority getting their way is what democracy is all about.

The House of Representatives should add additional members. The chamber has not added any seats in over one hundred years. The American population has increased around two hundred million people since then. That means that the population almost tripled in the last 100 years. In spite of that, the number of representatives in the House of Representatives has stayed the same. The American people are not nearly as well represented as they used to be. This may be partly why a lot of Americans today feel that their government ignores them and does not reflect their views. The American people are also not represented equally in the House of Representatives. Some members of the House represent around half a million people while others represent a million people or more. People would be angry if they discovered that their police protection or fire department protection varied depending on where they lived. How is it fair that people have a different level of representation in Congress depending on where they live? There should be more people serving in the House so that the people are more equally represented. To put up a number, there should be three times the number of members that we have now. That would be 1,305 members in the House of Representatives to accomplish this. Having a higher number of Representatives in Congress would be more democratic. The people would have representatives that were more responsive to their needs and desires. Politicians would have to work harder to earn the trust of their constituents. Having more representatives would also dilute the influence of special interests, corporations, and others who seek to influence the Congress. Governors and legislators should not be the architects and deciders of redistricting. There is an obvious conflict of interest to have the politicians deciding what the legislative and congressional districts look like. There should be a non-partisan process where the decision is taken out of the politicians hands. There could be a non-partisan committee elected by the people. Once that committee makes it recommendations, their proposals go before the voters for final approval. Or the voters themselves could propose what the state and congressional districts looked like and the competing proposals could go before the voters. The proposal that received the highest number of votes would become law. This would take an enormous amount of power out of the hands of politicians and give it to the people. It would also be a crucial step in making Congress more responsive and better representatives to their constituents. Adding members to the House of Representatives and changing the redistricting process would make America more democratic. It would take power away from Washington DC and the politicians in state capitals and give it to the American voters. In the next chapter I will talk about how we can achieve the goals outlined in this book.

# Chapter Nine

This book has outlined some ideas as to how to make America more democratic and how to solve some problems with the country. This chapter will review those ideas and discuss how they could happen. Ideas are one thing, but the real question is could any of these ideas actually happen? The end of this chapter will detail the two possible ways and the most likely method will be endorsed. Just to review the steps that America could take to become a democracy, the country should have a direct democracy. The people should get to propose laws and vote on them. We should not have the United States Senate anymore. That body is undemocratic and often stands in the way of what the people want. There should be term limits for members of Congress. Any member should not be allowed to serve for decades at a time. Members of the Supreme Court and federal courts should be subjected to term limits and elections. The people should get to decide who serves on the Supreme Court and the Federal Courts. Members of the Federal Reserve Board and the Federal Reserve district boards should be subjected to term limits and elections too. The banks and politicians should not be the sole deciders of such an important and powerful part of the Federal Government. We should get rid of the Electoral College. It's not democratic and it should not get in the way of the peoples decision. Political parties should hold their primaries for President on the same day throughout the country. We should increase the number of representatives that are serving in the House of Representatives. State legislatures and Governors should not be permitted to make congressional and legislative districts. The politicians have too much power in creating safe districts for members of their party. All of these reforms and ideas may very well be a waste of time if there is no way to make these things happen. There are two ways that one or all of these ideas could happen. The first would be for the constitutional amendment process to take place. The second way things could happen would be for a constitutional convention to be called.

The United States should have a direct democracy. That would mean that the people would be able to propose a law, collect the necessary number of voter signatures for it to be on the ballot and then the American people would be able to vote yes or no for that particular law. If the majority of people vote yes, the proposed law becomes law. If a majority of the people vote no, the proposed law does not become law. This would allow the American people to propose virtually any law that they wanted to propose. Another option available would be that multiple proposals would be before the voters at the same time. They would have multiple choices instead of just a Yes or No vote. The proposal or law that received the highest number of votes wins. Multiple proposals for anything from tax code reform, to healthcare reform to social security reform could go before the voters at the same time. This would allow the people to have multiple choices when they were considering a new law. Some issues are yes or no decisions while others require more complex answers and choices. This would give the people more power to tailor laws and the federal government to their liking and they could consider competing proposals at the same time. Multiple choices will end up giving the people the most options without compromising the ability to get anything done. If the people didn't like any of the proposals then they could vote to keep things the way that they are. The people would not be allowed to vote to bring back slavery, get rid of the right to vote, eliminate the constitution, etc. Laws passed would have to be constitutional. The people would be able to vote to amend the constitution through the traditional process or they could choose to change the way amendments are added to the Constitution. This experiment of direct democracy has already taken hold in half of American states along with the District of Columbia. They have not voted to make some person dictator or secede from the union. The outrageous proposals are most often never on the ballot in the first place. If they somehow receive enough voter signatures to appear on the ballot, then they most often lose. If the voters were to approve of a law that was in violation of the Constitution and or federal law, there very well could be a court challenge. The issue could even end up being decided by the US Supreme Court. If a law passed that was instantly unpopular or became unpopular, to get rid of it would require two thirds of the members of the House of Representatives and (if there still is a Senate) two thirds of the members of the US Senate to vote to get rid of a law. It's either the Congress or the Supreme Court that would have the ability to get rid of a law passed by the people. That would be a contingency in the event that the people demanded it, or if serious constitutional issues arose from passing a law. Direct democracy would put the American people in the driver seat of the federal government. They would get to decide what issues were important to them, vote on them, and pass what they felt was good for the nation. They would not have to be held hostage by politicians, Republicans, Democrats, corporations, special interests, lobbyists, and other groups and people that have heavy influence in Washington. They would be able to circumvent that entire process of DC and pass what they wanted. The American people are sick of being ignored, they are sick of being denied common sense solutions to their problems and they are sick of partisanship.

The United State Senate is not a democratic body and the Senate unfairly represents the American people. The Senate is full of career politicians that have too much power and stay in Washington for too long. The United States Senate should be done away with. The body slows down the Congress and was created to do that very thing. The Senate stifles the American peoples will for change. The Senate has become an aristocracy in the United States with a record number of Senators being millionaires and many of them end up serving for decades. The Senate was created to slow down the peoples influence and to create an even relationship amongst the states. Yet it is unfair that a Senator from Wyoming represents around five hundred thousand people and a California Senator represents over thirty-five million people. The Senate does not fairly represent the people and their interests. If there were just a House of Representatives, it would mean the people would have more of a say in the affairs of Washington. The Senate just like the Electoral College was created out of the necessity of creating the Republic. Colonies with smaller populations did not want to join a new country where colonies with large populations would dominate them and make it so they had no say or influence. In order to make smaller colonies agree to join the new country a compromise was reached. There would be a House of Representatives to give the large states a larger share of power that they wanted. But the Senate was created to make all of the states equal. Each state would get two members of the Senate. The Senate was created for the states and in the beginning every state legislature got to choose who their senators were. Americans didn't get to elect their US Senators until the progressive era in the late 19th and early 20th centuries. Making America into a democracy would require less power for the federal government as well as the states. That power would go to the American people.

We should have term limits for members of Congress. For members of the House of Representatives, they are elected to a two-year term in office. They can serve as long as they would like to, given that they keep getting re-elected every two years. There are many members of the House of Representatives that have been serving for decades. In the United States Senate, members are elected to six-year terms in office. They can serve as long as they would like too, as long as they keep getting re-elected. There are many members of the Senate that have been in office for decades. Members of Congress end up serving for many years, sometimes even until their death. Why is it fair that the President can only serve for two four-year terms in office while members of Congress can serve as long as they like? Is it fair to other people that are perfectly qualified to serve in Congress that members serve for so long that they never get the chance? The people are not being served as well as the members of the Congress are for being able to serve for so many years. Members who serve in Congress for many years are captured by special interest groups, their political party, lobbyists and the ways of Washington in general. They tend to forget about those they are supposed to represent rather quickly. Members in the House of Representatives should still have two-year terms. Yet they should only serve in the House for a maximum of four terms that would total eight years. Senators should have four-year terms instead of six-year terms and they should only be able to serve for two terms that would total a maximum of eight years (This is all of course if there still is a Senate). If the President can only serve for eight years, the same rule should apply to members of Congress. Term limits would help deter career politicians, it would erode the special interests influence in Congress and it would continually introduce new people into Congress. The American people would be better served by a constantly new and responsive Congress, rather than a Congress made up of career politicians that play partisan games and owe their loyalty to the special interests that give them campaign cash that helps keep them in Congress for decades.

There should be term limits for those serving on the US Supreme Court and federal courts and those serving should be elected. The judges serving on other federal courts such as courts of appeals and district courts should also be subjected to term limits and elections. Judges in federal courts throughout the United States have a lot of power and the people have little to no influence or control over them. The President is the only person who gets to decide who is even allowed to be a federal judge or serve on the Supreme Court. The members of the US Senate are the only people that get to vote as to whether someone is allowed to serve on Federal courts. The power that the President and the Senators have should be given to the American people. It would make America more democratic to be able to decide who is serving on the federal courts. It would make judges more in tune with the people and it would allow any person to become a federal judge. Elections would open up the process so a long list of qualified people would be able to serve that do not share the President and Senators political opinions. Electing federal judges would also mean that they were less controlled by special interests than they are today. Many judges serve on courts for decades, since they serve for so long, they should be subjected to two terms. Each term should be four years long; somebody could serve as a federal judge for eight years, an appellate court judge for eight years and on the Supreme Court for eight years. Members of the Federal courts would be elected in staggered terms. Some judges would be up for re-election every two years instead of all of them every four years. Members of the Supreme Court would be running in national elections where everyone in America could vote. For federal courts in districts or geographic regions of the country, only the people who lived in that district or area would be able to elect people to that Appellate Court. Electing other federal judges would be a citywide or more local election. For such a powerful branch of the federal government, the American people have little or no influence over it. The federal judiciary is the third branch of the federal government but the people have no control over it. We are able to elect people to Congress and the White House, why not the federal judicial system? Judges in federal courts should be elected and be subjected to term limits. The sole deciders of who get's to serve on federal courts should not be up to the President and members of the Senate, it should be the American people who get to decide. The members of federal courts should not be permitted to serve indefinitely on the Court either. They should have term limits and not be confirmed once and never receive any scrutiny again.

Members of the United States Federal Reserve should be elected and be subjected to term limits. Members of regional Federal Reserve boards should be subjected to elections and term limits as well. The people that live in Federal Reserve districts would get to vote for whom they wanted to serve on their regions Federal Reserve board. The banks and politicians in Washington should not be the people who decide who serves on regional Federal Reserve boards. Everyone in the country would be able to vote for people that were running to serve on the Federal Reserve board in Washington DC. The Federal Reserve was created around one hundred years ago and there is noting in the Constitution that says how the Federal Reserve board should function. It is such a large and powerful institution that the American people have no control over. The people should be able to have a check against the Federal Reserve. If the people could elect members of the Federal Reserve, they could assure that members serve their interests over that of banks and politicians. The Federal Reserve is extremely influential in setting interest rates, dealing with inflation, the money supply and dealing with the economy in general. Our very economic fortunes depend upon the Federal Reserve getting it right when it comes to the economy. That's way too much power for an opaque institution that the people have no way of controlling. Members of the Federal Reserve should be limited to serving for two terms and each term should be four years long. Each member would be elected to staggered terms. Making America more democratic would involve giving the American people control over the Federal Reserve. It is a large part of the Federal government that is almost as powerful as the legislative, executive, and judicial branches. Having elections would give any person the opportunity to serve in the Federal Reserve. It would not be limited to those that banks, politicians, and special interests in Washington would approve of.

We should get rid of the Electoral College. Political parties should hold all of their primaries for President on the same day. The Electoral College is not democratic. It was created at the beginning of the Republic as a way to decide who the President was. The popular vote for president was not counted until decades after the first presidential election. The Electoral College has not been that relevant in a lot of American history. Typically the person that won the popular vote for President won the Electoral College anyway. But there have been three times in American history when the presidential candidate lost the popular vote and won the Electoral College and became President, which happened in 1876, 1888, and in 2000. The Electoral College should not be able to overrule the American peoples will. Not to mention, there are about a dozen swing states that dominate the presidential campaign these days. The Electoral College gives these states way too much influence and attention during Presidential campaigns. Candidates for President should be forced to run a national campaign and not focus all of their campaigning and attention on a small number of states that decide the election only because of the Electoral College. The country does not need the Electoral College and the country would be more democratic without it. Political parties should be forced to have their primaries for President on the same day. That would allow all of the candidates to have an equal chance of getting the nomination. It would allow a greater variety of candidates to have the chance of getting nominated. Having a national primary on the same day would allow all members of each political party to have an equal say in determining who becomes their parties nominee. It would also be more fair to people who lived in states other than the early voting states. People who live in Iowa, New Hampshire, and South Carolina have far too much influence in deciding who the nominees for President are. People in all states should be equally represented and have an equal chance in deciding who their political parties nominee for President is.

We should increase the number of representatives in the House of Representatives. State legislatures and Governors should not be able to decide what state legislative and congressional districts look like. There are four hundred and thirty five members in the House of Representatives and this has remained unchanged for over one hundred years, yet the American population is three times larger than it was back then. The number of representatives in the House should be at least triple to keep up with the increase in the country's population of the last hundred years. Making America more democratic would involve increasing the number of representatives in Congress. It would be a body that would better represent the people and it would be a body that would be more responsive to the people and their desires. State legislatures and Governors should not be able to create legislative and congressional districts. There should be a non-partisan committee of people that get to decide what those districts look like. The districts that they propose should go up for approval by the voters. It should also be possible for the voters themselves to propose their own state and congressional districts. The proposal that received the highest number of votes would become law. This option would allow the voters to redistrict much more often than under the status quo where redistricting can only take place every ten years after the Census. The people that live in each state should have the final say as to what these state and congressional districts look like. The power of redistricting should be taken out of the hands of politicians and put into the hands of the people.

The previous eight chapters have discussed ideas that would make the United States more democratic. Those ideas may be the foundation for what could make America a genuinely democratic country. At the moment, the United States is a republic. It is governed by the United States Constitution and still would be if the democratic reforms proposed became apart of the Constitution. These proposed reforms would take power out of the hands of politicians in Washington, the President, the Congress, the Federal Reserve, The Supreme Court, the federal judicial system, the states, as well as the special interests and lobbyists in Washington DC. The power that all of these groups currently possess would go to the American people. That is the main goal of the ideas presented in this book. The people would be able to continue the work of making America more democratic with new ideas and the ability to keep presenting new laws that would make their government more to their liking. The ideas presented in this book are merely a starting point. The people would be able to do what they wanted to do. Some may like none of the ideas; some may like all of the ideas in this book. It's up to the American people whether they think one or any of these ideas are good for them, much less for the country. The theme of this book is democracy and the people should be the ultimate deciders of what kind of a federal government that they want. They should have the power to decide what kind of a relationship that they want with Washington.

Having all of the ideas presented in this book may be good or even interesting. These ideas are all for nothing if they could not happen in the real world. The ideas in this book would not be as interesting if there was no clear way to turn these ideas into action. How would any of these things actually happen in the real world? How could any of these things actually happen in the United States? There are two general ways that these ideas could be put into practice in the United States. Since the ideas presented in this book are so large, most of them would have to involve changing the US Constitution. Making America into a direct democracy, getting rid of the US Senate, imposing term limits on members of Congress and the Supreme Court. These things among others would require amending the Constitution and there is no other way that these ideas could happen other than that. The Constitution says that there are two general ways to amend the constitution. The first way to make changes occur would be to amend the Constitution. There have been twenty-seven amendments to the Constitution throughout American history so far. These amendments have consisted of everything from the Bill of Rights to the thirteenth amendment that eliminated slavery. How is an amendment to the Constitution made? A member of Congress must propose an amendment first. After that happens, a proposed amendment must be taken up to a vote by the members of the House of Representatives. For an amendment to get through the House of Representatives, it would require over two thirds of the members to vote in favor of an amendment. That is two thirds of the four hundred and thirty-five members. At least two hundred and ninety members of the House of Representatives have to vote in favor of an amendment. After that happens, the proposed amendment goes to the United States Senate. This requires that the proposed amendment be allowed to go up for a vote in the Senate. Those in the leadership of the Senate have to allow a vote to occur. Once that happens, it would require two thirds of the members of the Senate to vote in favor of a proposed amendment. This would mean that at least sixty-seven senators out of one hundred would have to vote in favor of a proposed amendment. If at least sixty-seven Senators vote in favor of a proposed Constitutional amendment, then it must go to the states. The state legislatures would get to vote on the proposed amendment. For the amendment to be approved by a state, it would require the states House of Representatives and States Senate to vote in favor. When three out of four states or 38/50 of the state legislatures vote in favor of a proposed amendment it becomes an amendment to the United States Constitution. Ideas presented in this book would have to be proposed one at a time in this process. You could not put all of the ideas presented in this book into one amendment; it would require at least seven separate amendments to the constitution. It is not necessary to have a constitutional amendment for things such as making the Federal Reserve have term limits and members being forced to be elected. The Federal Reserve is not in the constitution so it is not necessary to amend it to change it. Making states change the way they redistrict may or may not be constitutional. Increasing the number of representatives in the House of Representatives would not require an amendment either.

The second way for a constitutional amendment to pass would be for the states to call for a constitutional convention. This would require two thirds of the state legislatures to vote in favor of a constitutional convention. There has not been one since the original Constitutional Convention in 1787, which is when the US Constitution was written. For this to happen again it would require at least thirty-four out of fifty state legislatures to call for one. That would allow the amendments to be added to the Constitution that the people wanted. This would be a way of enacting some, or all of the ideas presented in this book. It would give the American people the ability to decide other changes that they would like to make to the Constitution. The Constitutional convention would help the American people decide the things that they wanted to change. A Constitutional Convention would allow the amendments proposed in this book to take place. All of the states would get to participate in the constitutional convention; this would be all the more appropriate when you consider that most states did not exist in the 1780s. A constitutional convention today would allow all 50 states to participate along with the American public, so every state could have input along with the people.

In the 1780's the Articles of Confederation governed the country. It was a relatively weak document that left a small federal government. There were efforts to create a stronger document; Alexander Hamilton and James Madison led a group to persuade George Washington that there should be a constitutional convention. Washington supported those efforts which led to the Annapolis Convention in 1786 to petition Congress to call a constitutional convention to meet in Philadelphia. A few state representatives met to declare their support to improve upon the Articles of Confederation. The states representatives in Philadelphia met in secret closed door sessions and wrote a new constitution. The new one gave the federal government much more power and the representatives wanted to create a government as close to a republic as possible. They also wanted to address the various problems that were occurring between the states. The US government was a totally new kind of government; it was a mix of a centralized government and a confederation of sovereign states. Every other government in the world was either a centralized government or a confederation of sovereign states. In light of Shays Rebellion, which almost succeeded in bringing down the state government of Massachusetts, more favored a stronger federal government. States were having difficulty collecting taxes, paying their revolutionary war debt and governing a war weary population. Landholders favored a stronger federal government to facilitate land deals in the west. The Continental Congress had difficulty passing much national policy and had no powers to tax or to collect tariffs. American manufacturers wanted high tariffs but were unable to get that without a stronger federal government. The Articles of Confederation required every state to approve of a change to the articles in order for anything to change, whereas the new constitution stated that only nine states were needed to ratify the constitution. Since the Constitution was a completely new document the rules under the Articles of Confederation didn't matter anymore. On May 14th 1787 the Virginia and Pennsylvania delegations met in Philadelphia and began working on a new constitution, on May 25th five other state delegations joined them. There were twelve states with 74 delegates named to go to the Convention. Of the 74 delegates 55 attended and 39 delegates actually signed the Constitution. The delegates debated amongst each other over issues like national government, foreign affairs, the economy, the relationship between states and the new federal government. The delegates were heavily influenced by Age of Enlightenment philosophers like John Locke, Edward Coke, Montesquieu and Immanuel Kant who advocated for liberty, freedom, the triumph of reason and free thought from religious authorities. At the convention there was the Virginia Plan, which was proposed by the Virginia delegation, this plan proposed a bicameral legislature that would have given each state a number of representatives in Congress based off of their population. Virginia was one of the most populated states so this would have benefited them. The New Jersey Plan which was proposed by the New Jersey delegation a single chamber legislature where each state would have equal representation regardless of population. This led to what was called the Connecticut Compromise, which created the House of Representatives based off of population, and the Senate which gives each state equal representation. The convention called for a federal government with three branches, legislative, executive and judicial. These would be known as the checks and balances of our system that ensures that one branch cannot be more powerful than any other branch. If one branch becomes too powerful the other two branches check them. The five men elected to write a detailed constitution were John Rutledge, Oliver Ellsworth, James Wilson, Nathanial Gorham and Edmund Randolph; this group was called the committee of detail. Those men met in July 24th 1787 to begin creating the document, meanwhile the Constitution Convention recessed from July 26th to August 6th. From August 6th to September 10th the Constitutional Convention reconvened to go over the written constitution of the committee of detail. On September 8th a committee of style of five people was selected to close the discussions and create the final document. There were seven articles plus a preamble that created the rules for governing the United States. Not all were pleased with what they had created; Benjamin Franklin begrudgingly accepted the new document and signed it. Eleven state delegations had approved of the new Constitution and Alexander Hamilton as New Yorks sole delegate also approved. After the Constitutional Convention was concluded the Constitution was sent to the continental Congress in New York City and then it was given to that states to ask for ratification. Each state legislature would get to decide if they would ratify the new constitution or not. Eleven states quickly ratified the Constitution, North Carolina and Rhode Island did so by May 1790. There was heated debate about the new Constitution; there were the Federalists who supported the new Constitution and the Anti-Federalists who opposed it. Alexander Hamilton, James Madison and John Jay authored the Federalist papers, which were a series of essays that supported ratifying the new Constitution. The Federalist papers are used by legal scholars as well as the Supreme Court to determine the true intent behind provisions in the Constitution. There was a very contentious battle between the Federalists and the Anti-Federalists; the Federalists were more united so they succeeded at convincing the states to ratify the Constitution. The Articles of Confederation continued to govern the country until September 15th 1788 when the ninth state ratified the Constitution. On March 4th 1789 was the first day that Congress began its first session. George Washington was inaugurated on April 30th 1789 in New York City (New York was the capital) and the new government took over from the continental congress.

Article V of the American Constitution allows for an amendment proposing convention. Each state would send delegates to this convention and changes to the Constitution would be proposed and voted on. It would require two thirds of the states to vote in favor of a constitutional convention in order for one to happen. When that happens it would be called the Article V Convention. At this convention, three fourths or seventy five percent of the states would have to vote in favor of a proposed amendment for it to become apart of the Constitution. There have been calls to hold a second constitutional convention in recent years. Whether it has been proposed for a balanced budget amendment or to change the constitution entirely. A lot of calls have been made in recent years to change the Constitution and around thirty states have already called for a constitutional convention. This is a second way that some of the changes in this book could actually take place. Either by having an amendment to the Constitution just like the prior twenty-seven amendments have been done. Or there could be a constitutional convention held and many things would be up for consideration all at once. Considering that one of the proposed changes include getting rid of the United States Senate, it won't be possible to pass an amendment in the traditional process. The only way for the ideas in this book to happen would be for a constitutional convention. The American public would have to put pressure on their state legislatures and demand a constitutional convention. Since so many states have already called for one, it would not take a lot of work to get several more states to call for one. One of the reasons why a constitutional convention hasn't happened yet is because there has not been a consensus as to why we need to have one. Making America into a democracy may be the series of amendments that finally causes enough states to call for a constitutional convention. The American people should be the ones in charge of their federal government. In the beginning the country had strong states and a weak federal government. Today America has weak states and a far too powerful federal government. The people deserve an increase in their power commensurate with how powerful the federal government has become. All of the centralized power in Washington needs to be decentralized. America was created as a republic and is still that way. Enacting the proposed changes in this book would make America into a democracy. It would allow the American people to control their own federal government. They would no longer have to wait around for the right kind person to become President; they would be empowered to govern themselves at long last in freedom.

# Sources Cited

"Encyclopedia.com | Free Online Encyclopedia." Web. 6 Mar 2015. <http://encyclopedia.com>.

OpenStax College, . US History. OpenStax College, 2014. Print.

Delegates of ConstitutionalConvention, . Pocket Constituion.2nd. National Center for Constitutional Studies, 2005. Print.

Alexander, Hamilton, James Madison, John Jay and Clinton Rossiter. The Federalist Papers . 1st. Signet, Print.

Patrick, Henry, Samuel Byron and Robert Yates. The Anti-Federalist Papers. CreateSpace Independent Publishing Platform, 2010. Print.

Thomas, Paine. Common Sense. Dover Publications, 1997. Print.

Joseph, Ellis. The Quartet: Orchestrating the Second American Revolution, 1783-1789. 1st. Knopf, 2015. Print.

Jonathan, Hughes and Louis Cain. American Economic History.8th. Prentice Hall, 2010. Print.

John Steele, Gordon. An Empire of Wealth: The Epic History of American Economic Power. Reprint. Harper Perennial, 2005. Print.

James, Olson and Abraham Mendoza. American Economic History: A Dictionary and Chronology. Greenwood, 2015. Print.

Samuel, Kernell and Steven Smith. Principles and Practice of American Politics: Classic and Contemporary Readings. 6th. Sage Publications Inc, 2015. Print.

Gary, Wasserman. The Basics of American Politics. 15th. Pearson, 2014. Print.

Riley, Peake. Mapping Census 2010: The Geography of American Change . Esri Press, 2012. Print.

Milton, Friedman. Capitalism and Freedom. University Of Chicago Press, 1962. Print.

Bernard, Schwartz. A History of the Supreme Court. Reprint. Oxford University Press, 1995. Print.

Gary, Hartman, Roy Mersky and Cindy Tate. Landmark Supreme Court Cases: The Most Influential Decisions of the Supreme Court of the United States. Facts on File, 2004. Print.

Catherine McGrew, Jaime. Understanding Presidential Elections: The Constitution, Caucuses, Primaries, Electoral College, and More. CreateSpace Independent Publishing Platform, 2012. Print.

Lawerance, Longley and Neal R. Peirce. The Electoral College Primer 2000. Yale University Press, 1999. Print.

David O., Stewart. He Summer of 1787: The Men Who Invented the Constitution. Simon & Schuster, 2008. Print.

Presidential Elections 1789-2008. 10. CQ Press, 2009. Print.

Marc J., Schulman. A History of American Presidential Elections: From George Washington to Barack Obama. Multi Educator, 2012. Print.

Charles S, Bullock III. Redistricting: The Most Political Activity in America. Rowman & Littlefield Publishers, 2010. Print.

Jonathan, Winburn. The Realities of Redistricting: Following the Rules and Limiting Gerrymandering in State Legislative Redistricting. Lexington Books, 2009. Print.

Allen, Smith. Money, Banking and The Federal Reserve System.2011. Ebook.

Donald, Wells. The Federal Reserve System: A History.McFarland, 2004. Print.

E. Victor, Morgan. The Theory and Practice of Central Banking, 1797-1913. Cambridge University Press, 1943. Print.

Winton U., Solberg. The Constitutional Convention and Formation of Union. 2nd. University of Illinois Press, 1990. Print.

Max, Farrand. The Records of the Federal Convention of 1787.Revised. One. Yale University Press, 1966. Print.

John R., Vile. Essential Supreme Court Decisions: Summaries of Leading Cases in U.S. Constitutional Law. 15th. Rowman & Littlefield Publishers, 2010. Print.

Richard H., Fallon Jr., John F. Manning, Daniel J. Meltzer and David L. Sharpiro. The Federal Courts and the Federal System.6th. Foundation Press, 2009. Print.

Barbara, Norrander. The Imperfect Primary: Oddities, Biases, and Strengths of U.S. Presidential Nomination Politics (Controversies in Electoral Democracy and Representation). 1st. Routledge, 2010. Print.